THE DEVELOPMENT

OF

PERSONALITY

C. G. JUNG

TRANSLATED BY R. F. C. HULL

ROUTLEDGE & KEGAN PAUL

LONDON AND HENLEY

FIRST PUBLISHED IN ENGLAND IN 1954
BY ROUTLEDGE & KEGAN PAUL, LTD.
39 STORE STREET
LONDON WC1E 7DD AND
BROADWAY HOUSE, NEWTOWN ROAD
HENLEY-ON-THAMES, OXON RG9 1EN

REPRINTED IN USA 1965 AND 1971
FIRST PRINTED IN GREAT BRITAIN 1977

PRINTED BY UNWIN BROTHERS LIMITED
THE GRESHAM PRESS, OLD WOKING, SURREY, ENGLAND
A MEMBER OF THE STAPLES PRINTING GROUP

THIS EDITION IS BEING PUBLISHED
BY ROUTLEDGE & KEGAN PAUL, LTD., IN ENGLAND
AND FOR THE BOLLINGEN FOUNDATION BY PANTHEON BOOKS INC.
IN THE UNITED STATES OF AMERICA.
THE PRESENT VOLUME IS NUMBER 17 OF THE COLLECTED WORKS,
AND WAS THE FOURTH TO APPEAR.

ISBN 0 7100 1646 8

EDITORIAL NOTE

Personality as the expression of the wholeness of man is defined by Jung as an adult ideal whose conscious realization through individuation is the aim of human development in the second half of life. It is to the study of this aim that Jung has devoted his main attention in all his later work. It is manifest that in childhood and adolescence the ego is brought into being and firmly established; no account of individuation, therefore, would be complete without a psychological outline of the early formative period of development.

The present volume is a collection of Professor Jung's papers on child psychology and education, of which the three lectures on "Analytical Psychology and Education" are the chief item. Jung regards the psychology of parents and educators as of the greatest importance in the maturation and growth to consciousness of the children—especially so in the case of those who are unusually gifted. He emphasizes that an unsatisfactory psychological relationship between the parents may be an important cause of psychogenic disorders in childhood. It has been thought relevant to include Jung's paper on "Marriage as a Psychological Relationship" and, finally, to link up the problems of childhood with those of individuation in the adult by adding the essay which gives the present volume its title.

The essay "Child Development and Education" is presented here for the first time under this title. It previously appeared as one of the four lectures on "Analytical Psychology and Education," published in *Contributions to Analytical Psychology;* yet it had been delivered on a different occasion from the three others, its subject-matter is different, and it is not included by Jung in *Psychologie und Erziehung,* which contains the three other lectures. It contains a significant textual change by the author: an important statement in paragraph 106 on the subject

v

of archetypal images in the dreams of children. Editorial reference is given to the privately printed record of Jung's seminars on the subject.

Only the essay "The Gifted Child" and the introduction to Frances Wickes's book *Analyse der Kinderseele* have not previously been translated into English, apart from the brief alteration mentioned above. But the author has considerably revised the essays on education, so that much new matter is to be found in this volume, which will, it is hoped, help to set forth Jung's position in regard to child psychology.

TRANSLATOR'S NOTE

With the exception of the "Introduction to Wickes's *Analyse der Kinderseele*" and "The Gifted Child," all the papers in the present volume were previously translated by various hands and published in *Collected Papers on Analytical Psychology* (2nd edition, London, 1917, and New York, 1920), *Contributions to Analytical Psychology* (London and New York, 1928), and *The Integration of the Psychology* (New York, 1939; London, 1940). Several of them, as indicated in the footnotes at the beginning of each paper, have since been revised and expanded by the author. I would like to express my thanks to the late Dr. A. A. Brill, Mr. Stanley Dell, and in particular to Mrs. Cary F. Baynes, for permission to make full use of the earlier texts in preparing the present revised versions.

TABLE OF CONTENTS

I

PSYCHIC CONFLICTS IN A CHILD

[The third of a series of lectures on "The Association Method," delivered on the 20th anniversary of the opening of Clark University, Worcester, Massachusetts, September, 1909. The original version was published under the title "Über Konflikte der kindlichen Seele," *Jahrbuch für psychoanalytische und psychopathologische Forschungen*, II (1910), 33ff. It was translated by A. A. Brill and published in the *American Journal of Psychology*, XXI (1910), in a Clark University anniversary volume (1910), and in *Collected Papers on Analytical Psychology* (1st ed., London, 1916; 2nd ed., London, 1917, and New York, 1920). The revised version, of which this present essay is a translation, appeared in *Psychologie und Erziehung* (Zurich, 1946).—EDITORS.]

FOREWORD TO THE SECOND EDITION

I am publishing this little study just as it is, without making any alterations for the second edition. Although in point of fact our conceptions have been considerably modified and extended since these observations first appeared in 1910, I do not feel that the subsequent modifications would justify me in describing the views put forward in the first edition as basically false, an imputation that has been laid against me in certain quarters. On the contrary, just as the observations here recorded have retained their value as facts, so also have the conceptions themselves. But no conception is ever all-embracing, for it is always dominated by a point of view. The point of view adopted in this work is psycho-biological. It is naturally not the only one possible, indeed there are several others. Thus, more in accord with the spirit of Freudian psychology, this little piece of child psychology could be regarded from the purely hedonistic standpoint, the psychological process being conceived as a movement dominated by the pleasure principle. The main motives would then be the desire for and the striving towards the most pleasurable, and hence the most satisfying, realization of fantasy. Or, following Adler's suggestion, one could regard the same material from the standpoint of the power principle, an approach which is psychologically just as legitimate as that of the hedonistic principle. Or one could employ a purely logical approach,

3

with the intention of demonstrating the development of logical processes in the child. One could even approach the matter from the standpoint of the psychology of religion and give prominence to the earliest beginnings of the God-concept. I have been content to steer a middle course that keeps to the psycho-biological method of observation, without attempting to subordinate the material to this or that hypothetical key principle. In so doing I am not, of course, contesting the legitimacy of such principles, for they are all included in our human nature; but only a very one-sided specialist would think of declaring as universally valid the heuristic principle that had proved its particular value for his discipline or for his individual method of observation. The essence of human psychology, precisely because so many different possible principles exist, can never be fully comprehended under any one of them, but only under the totality of individual aspects.

The basic hypothesis of the view advanced in this work is that sexual interest plays a not inconsiderable role in the nascent process of infantile thinking, an hypothesis that should meet with no serious opposition. A contrary hypothesis would certainly come up against too many well-observed facts, quite apart from its being extraordinarily improbable that a fundamental instinct of such cardinal importance for human psychology should not make itself felt in the infantile psyche from the very beginning.

On the other hand I also lay stress on the significance of *thinking* and the importance of concept-building for the solution of psychic conflicts. It should be sufficiently clear from what follows that the initial sexual interest strives only figuratively towards an immediate sexual goal, but far more towards the development of thinking. Were this not so, the solution of the conflict could be reached solely through the attainment of a sexual goal, and not through the mediation of an intellectual concept. But precisely the latter is the case, from which we may conclude that infantile sexuality is not to be identified outright with adult sexuality, since adult sexuality cannot be adequately replaced by concept-building, but is in most cases only satisfied with the real sexual goal, namely the tribute of normal sexual functioning which nature exacts. On the other hand, we know from experience that the infantile beginnings of sexuality can

4

also lead to real sexual functioning—masturbation—when the conflicts are not resolved. The building of concepts, however, opens out to the libido a channel that is capable of further development, so that its continual, active realization is assured. Given a certain intensity of conflict, the absence of concept-building acts as a hindrance which thrusts the libido back into its initial sexuality, with the result that these beginnings or buddings are brought prematurely to an abnormal pitch of development. This produces an infantile neurosis. Gifted children in particular, whose mental demands begin to develop early on account of their intelligent disposition, run a serious risk of premature sexual realization through the suppression of what their parents and teachers would call an unsuitable curiosity.

As these reflections show, I do not regard the thinking function as just a makeshift function of sexuality which sees itself hindered in its pleasurable realization and is therefore compelled to pass over into the thinking function; but, while perceiving in infantile sexuality the beginnings of a future sexual function, I also discern there the seeds of higher spiritual functions. The fact that infantile conflicts can be resolved through concept-building speaks in favour of this, and also the fact that even in adult life the vestiges of infantile sexuality are the seeds of vital spiritual functions. The fact that adult sexuality grows out of this polyvalent germinal disposition does not prove that infantile sexuality is "sexuality" pure and simple. I therefore dispute the rightness of Freud's idea of the "polymorphous-perverse" disposition of the child. It is simply a *polyvalent* disposition. If we proceeded according to the Freudian formula, we should have to speak, in embryology, of the ectoderm as the brain, because from it the brain is ultimately developed. But much also develops from it besides the brain, for instance the sense organs and other things.

December, 1915   C. G. J.

FOREWORD TO THE THIRD EDITION

Since this paper first appeared, almost thirty years have gone by. Yet it would seem that this little work has not given up the ghost, but is in increasing demand with the public. In one or two respects, certainly, it has never grown stale, firstly because it presents a simple series of facts such as occur repeatedly and are found to be much the same everywhere; secondly because it demonstrates something of great practical and theoretical importance, namely the characteristic striving of the child's fantasy to outgrow its "realism" and to put a "symbolic" interpretation in the place of scientific rationalism. This striving is evidently a natural and spontaneous expression of the psyche, which for that very reason cannot be traced back to any "repression" whatsoever. I stressed this particular point in my Foreword to the second edition, and my mention of it there has not lost its topicality, since the myth of the polymorphous sexuality of the child is still sedulously believed in by the majority of specialists. The repression theory is as grossly overestimated as ever, while the natural phenomena of psychic transformation are accordingly underestimated, if not entirely ignored. In 1912, I made these phenomena the subject of a compendious study, which cannot be said even now to have penetrated the intellects of psychologists as a class. I trust therefore that the present modest and factual report will succeed in rousing the reader to

6

reflection. Theories in psychology are the very devil. It is true that we need certain points of view for their orienting and heuristic value; but they should always be regarded as mere auxiliary concepts that can be laid aside at any time. We still know so very little about the psyche that it is positively grotesque to think we are far enough advanced to frame general theories. We have not even established the empirical extent of the psyche's phenomenology: how then can we dream of general theories? No doubt theory is the best cloak for lack of experience and ignorance, but the consequences are depressing: bigotedness, superficiality, and scientific sectarianism.

To document the polyvalent germinal disposition of the child with a sexual terminology borrowed from the stage of fully-fledged sexuality is a dubious undertaking. It means drawing everything else in the child's make-up into the orbit of sexual interpretation, so that on the one hand the concept of sexuality is blown up to fantastic proportions and becomes nebulous, while on the other hand spiritual factors are seen as warped and stunted instincts. Views of this kind lead to a rationalism which is not even remotely capable of doing justice to the essential polyvalence of the infantile disposition. Even though a child may be preoccupied with matters which, for adults, have an undoubtedly sexual complexion, this does not prove that the nature of the child's preoccupation is to be regarded as equally sexual. For the cautious and conscientious investigator sexual terminology, as applied to infantile phenomena, can be deemed at most a professional *façon de parler*. I have my qualms about its appropriateness.

Apart from a few small improvements I am allowing this paper to appear once again in unaltered form.

December, 1938   C. G. J.

PSYCHIC CONFLICTS IN A CHILD

1   About the time when Freud published his report on the case of "Little Hans," [1] I received from a father who was acquainted with psychoanalysis a series of observations concerning his little daughter, then four years old.

2   These observations have so much that bears upon, and supplements, Freud's report on "Little Hans" that I cannot refrain from making this material accessible to a wider public. The widespread incomprehension, not to say indignation, with which "Little Hans" was greeted, was for me an additional reason for publishing my material, although it is nothing like as extensive as that of "Little Hans." Nevertheless, it contains points which seem to confirm how typical the case of "Little Hans" is. So-called "scientific" criticism, so far as it has taken any notice at all of these important matters, has once more proved overhasty, seeing that people have still not learned first to examine and then to judge.

3   The little girl to whose sagacity and intellectual sprightliness we are indebted for the following observations is a healthy, lively child of emotional temperament. She has never been seriously ill, nor had she ever shown any trace of "nervous" symptoms.

[1] "Analysis of a Phobia in a Five-year-old Boy," *Collected Papers,* Vol. III (London, 1925; first published in 1909).

4   Livelier systematic interests awakened in the child about her third year; she began to ask questions and to spin wishful fantasies. In the report which now follows we shall, unfortunately, have to give up the idea of a consistent exposition, for it is made up of anecdotes which treat of one isolated experience out of a whole cycle of similar ones, and which cannot, therefore, be dealt with scientifically and systematically, but must rather take the form of a story. We cannot dispense with this mode of exposition in the present state of our psychology, for we are still a long way from being able in all cases to separate with unerring certainty what is curious from what is typical.

5   When the child, whom we will call Anna, was about three years old, she had the following conversation with her grand-mother:

"Granny, why are your eyes so dim?"

"Because I am old."

"But you will become young again?"

"Oh dear, no. I shall become older and older, and then I shall die."

"And what then?"

"Then I shall be an angel."

"And then you will be a baby again?"

6   The child found here a welcome opportunity for the provisional solution of a problem. For some time she had been in the habit of asking her mother whether she would ever have a real live doll, a baby brother, which naturally gave rise to the question of where babies come from. As such questions were asked quite spontaneously and unobtrusively, the parents attached no significance to them, but responded to them as lightly as the child herself seemed to ask them. Thus one day she was told the pretty story that children are brought by the stork. Anna had already heard somewhere a slightly more serious version, namely that children are little angels who live in heaven and are then brought down by the said stork. This theory seems to have become the point of departure for the little one's investigating activities. From the conversation with the grandmother it could be seen that this theory was capable of wide application; for it solved in a comforting manner not only the painful thought of dying, but at the same time the riddle of where children come from. Anna seemed to be saying to herself: "When somebody

9

dies he becomes an angel, and then he becomes a child." Solutions of this sort, which kill at least two birds with one stone, used to be tenaciously adhered to even in science, and cannot be undone in the child's mind without a certain amount of shock. In this simple conception there lie the seeds of the reincarnation theory, which, as we know, is still alive today in millions of human beings.[2]

7   Just as the birth of a little sister was the turning point in the history of "Little Hans," so in this case it was the arrival of a baby brother, which took place when Anna had reached the age of four. The problem of where children come from, hardly touched upon so far, now became topical. The mother's pregnancy had apparently passed unnoticed; that is to say, Anna had never made any observations on this subject. On the evening before the birth, when labour pains were just beginning, the child found herself in her father's room. He took her on his knee and said, "Tell me, what would you say if you got a little brother tonight?" "I would kill him," was the prompt answer. The expression "kill" looks very alarming, but in reality it is quite harmless, for "kill" and "die" in child language only mean to "get rid of," either actively or passively, as has already been pointed out a number of times by Freud. I once had to treat a fifteen-year-old girl who, under analysis, had a recurrent association, and kept on thinking of Schiller's "Song of the Bell." She had never really read the poem, but had once glanced through it, and could only remember something about a cathedral tower. She could recall no further details. The passage goes:

> From the tower
> The bell-notes fall
> Heavy and sad
> For the funeral. . . .
>
> Alas it is the wife and mother,
> Little wife and faithful mother,
> Whom the dark prince of the shadows
> Snatches from her spouse's arms. . . .

2 [In the light of Professor Jung's later researches these theories can be understood as based upon the archetype of rebirth, in the unconscious. Several other examples of archetypal activity are to be found in this essay.—EDITORS.]

8   She naturally loved her mother dearly and had no thought of her death, but on the other hand the present position was this: she had to go away with her mother for five weeks, staying with relatives; the year before, the mother had gone by herself, and the daughter (an only and spoilt child) was left at home alone with her father. Unfortunately this year it was the "little wife" who was being snatched from the arms of her spouse, whereas the daughter would greatly have preferred the "faithful mother" to be parted from her child.

9   On the lips of a child, therefore, "kill" is a perfectly harmless expression, especially when one knows that Anna used it quite promiscuously for all possible kinds of destruction, removal, demolition, etc. All the same this tendency is worth noting. (Compare the analysis of "Little Hans.")

10   The birth occurred in the early morning. When all traces of the birth had been removed, together with the bloodstains, the father went into the room where Anna slept. She awoke as he entered. He told her the news of the arrival of a little brother, which she took with a surprised and tense expression on her face. The father then picked her up and carried her into the bedroom. Anna threw a rapid glance at her rather wan-looking mother and then displayed something like a mixture of embarrassment and suspicion, as if thinking, "What's going to happen now?" She evinced hardly any pleasure at the sight of the new arrival, so that the cool reception she gave it caused general disappointment. For the rest of the morning she kept very noticeably away from her mother; this was the more striking, as normally she was always hanging around her. But once, when her mother was alone, she ran into the room, flung her arms round her neck and whispered hurriedly, "Aren't you going to die now?"

11   Something of the conflict in the child's soul is now revealed to us. The stork theory had obviously never caught on properly, but the fruitful rebirth hypothesis undoubtedly had, according to which a person helps a child into life by dying. Mama ought therefore to die. Why, then, should Anna feel any pleasure over the new arrival, of whom she was beginning to feel childishly jealous anyway? Hence, she had to assure herself at a favourable opportunity whether Mama was going to die or not. Mama did not die. With this happy issue, however, the rebirth theory re-

ceived a severe setback. How was it now possible to explain little brother's birth and the origins of children in general? There still remained the stork theory, which, though never expressly rejected, had been implicitly waived in favour of the rebirth hypothesis.[3] The next attempts at explanation unfortunately remained hidden from the parents, as the child went to stay with her grandmother for a few weeks. From the latter's report, however, it appears that the stork theory was much discussed, there being of course a tacit agreement to support it.

12   When Anna returned home she again displayed, on meeting her mother, the same mixture of embarrassment and suspicion as after the birth. The impression was quite explicit to both parents, though not explicable. Her behaviour towards the baby was very nice. Meantime a nurse had arrived, who made a deep impression on little Anna with her uniform—an extremely negative impression at first, as she evinced the greatest hostility towards her in all things. Thus nothing would induce her to let herself be undressed in the evenings and put to bed by this nurse. The reason for this resistance soon became clear in a stormy scene by the bedside of the little brother, when Anna shouted at the nurse, "That's not your little brother, he is mine!" Gradually, however, she became reconciled to the nurse and began to play nurse herself; she had to have her white cap and apron, nursing her little brother and her dolls in turn. In contrast to her former mood the present one was unmistakably elegiac and dreamy. She often sat for hours crouched under the table singing long stories to herself and making rhymes, partly incomprehensible, but consisting partly of wishful fantasies on

---

[3] One might ask at this point why one is justified in supposing at all that children of this age worry their heads about such theories. The answer is that children are intensely interested in all the sensuously perceptible things going on around them. This also shows itself in the well-known endless questions concerning the why and wherefore of everything. One has to put off the dun-coloured spectacles of our culture for a moment if one wants to understand the psychology of a child. For everybody the birth of a child is quite the most important event there can possibly be. For our civilized thinking, however, birth has lost much of its biological uniqueness, just as sex has done. But somewhere or other the mind must have stored up the correct biological valuations impressed upon it all through the ages. What could be more probable than that the child still has these valuations and makes no bones about showing them, before civilization spreads like a pall over his primitive thinking?

the "nurse" theme ("I am a nurse of the green cross"), and partly of distinctly painful feelings which were struggling for expression.

13   Here we meet with an important new feature in the little one's life: reveries, the first stirrings of poetry, moods of an elegiac strain—all of them things which are usually to be met with only at a later phase of life, at a time when the youth or maiden is preparing to sever the family tie, to step forth into life as an independent person, but is still inwardly held back by aching feelings of homesickness for the warmth of the family hearth. At such a time they begin weaving poetic fancies in order to compensate for what is lacking. To approximate the psychology of a four-year-old to that of the boy or girl approaching puberty may at first sight seem paradoxical; the affinity lies, however, not in the age but in the mechanism. The elegiac reveries express the fact that part of the love which formerly belonged, and should belong, to a real object, is now *introverted,* that is, it is turned inwards into the subject and there produces an increased fantasy activity.[4] Whence comes this introversion? Is it a psychological manifestation peculiar to this period, or does it come from a conflict?

14   On this point the following episode is enlightening. Anna disobeyed her mother more and more often, saying insolently, "I shall go back to Granny!"

"But I shall be sad if you leave me."

"Ah, but you've got baby brother."

15   The mother's reaction shows us what the child was really getting at with her threats to go away again: she obviously wanted to hear what her mother would say to her proposal, what her attitude was in general, and whether the little brother had not ousted her altogether from her mother's affection. One must

---

4 This process is altogether typical. When life comes up against an obstacle, so that no adaptation can be achieved and the transference of libido to reality is suspended, then an introversion takes place. That is to say, instead of the libido working towards reality there is an increased fantasy activity which aims at removing the obstacle, or at least removing it in fantasy, and this may in time lead to a practical solution. Hence the exaggerated sexual fantasies of neurotics, who in this way try to overcome their specific repression; hence also the typical fantasy of stammerers, that they really possess a great talent for eloquence. (That they have some claims in this respect is brought home to us by Alfred Adler's thoughtful studies on organ inferiority.)

not, however, fall for this transparent piece of trickery. The child could see and feel perfectly well that she was not stinted of anything essential in her mother's love, despite the existence of her baby brother. The veiled reproach she levels at her mother on that score is therefore unjustified, and to the trained ear this is betrayed by the slightly affected tone of voice. One often hears similar tones even with grown-up people. Such a tone, which is quite unmistakable, does not expect to be taken seriously and obtrudes itself all the more forcibly for that reason. Nor should the reproach be taken to heart by the mother, for it is merely the forerunner of other and this time more serious resistances. Not long after the conversation narrated above, the following scene took place:

Mother: "Come, we'll go into the garden."

Anna: "You're lying to me. Watch out if you're not telling the truth!"

Mother: "What are you thinking of? Of course I'm telling the truth."

Anna: "No, you are not telling the truth."

Mother: "You'll soon see whether I'm telling the truth: we are going into the garden this minute."

Anna: "Is that true? You're quite sure it's true? You're not lying?"

16 Scenes of this kind were repeated a number of times. But this time the tone was more vehement and insistent, and also the accent on the word "lie" betrayed something special which the parents did not understand; indeed they attributed far too little significance at first to the child's spontaneous utterances. In this they were only doing what all official education does. We do not usually listen to children at any stage of their careers; in all the essentials we treat them as *non compos mentis* and in all the unessentials they are drilled to the perfection of automatons. Behind resistances there always lies a question, a conflict, of which we hear soon enough at another time and on another occasion. But usually we forget to connect the thing heard with the resistances. Thus, on another occasion, Anna faced her mother with the awkward questions:

"I want to be a nurse when I grow up."

"That's what I wanted to be when I was a child."

"Why aren't you a nurse, then?"

14

"Well, because I am a mother instead, and so I have children of my own to nurse."

Anna (thoughtfully): "Shall I be a different woman from you? Shall I live in a different place? Shall I still talk with you?"

17   The mother's answer again shows where the child's question was leading.[5] Anna would obviously like to have a child to nurse, just as the nurse has. Where the nurse got the child from is quite clear, and Anna could get a child in the same way when she grew up. Why then wasn't Mama such a nurse—that is, how did she get the child if she didn't get it in the same way as the nurse? Anna could get a child just as the nurse had done, but how all that was going to be different in the future, or rather how she was going to be like her mother in the matter of getting children, was not so easy to see. Hence the thoughtful question "Shall I be a different woman from you?" Shall I be different in every way? The stork theory is evidently no good, the dying theory no less so, therefore one gets a child as the nurse, for example, got hers. In this natural way she, too, could get one; but how about the mother, who is no nurse and yet has children? Looking at the matter from this angle, Anna asks, "Why aren't you a nurse?"—meaning: why haven't you got your child in the plain, straightforward, natural way? This strangely indirect mode of interrogation is typical and may be connected with the child's hazy grasp of the problem, unless we are to assume a certain "diplomatic vagueness" prompted by a desire to evade direct questioning. Later we shall find evidence of this possibility.

18   Anna is therefore confronted with the question "Where does the child come from?" The stork did not bring it; Mama did not die; nor did Mama get it in the same way as the nurse. She has,

5 The somewhat paradoxical view that the aim of the child's question is to be sought in the mother's answer requires a little discussion. It is one of the greatest of Freud's services to psychology that he opened up again the whole questionableness of *conscious* motives. One consequence of repressing the instincts is that the importance of conscious thinking for action is boundlessly overestimated. According to Freud, the criterion for the psychology of the act is not the conscious motive, but the *result* of the act (the result being evaluated not physically but psychologically). This view sets the act in a new and biologically revealing light. I refrain from examples and shall content myself with observing that this view is extremely valuable for psychoanalysis both in principle and as regards interpretation.

however, asked this question before and was informed by her father that the stork brings children; but this is definitely not so, she has never been deceived on this point. Therefore Papa and Mama and all the others lie. This readily explains her mistrustful attitude at the birth and the reproaches levelled against her mother. But it also explains another point, namely the elegiac reveries which we have attributed to a partial introversion. We now know the real object from which love had to be withdrawn and introverted for lack of an aim: it was withdrawn from the parents who deceived her and refused to tell her the truth. (What can this be which must not be uttered? What goes on here? Such are the parenthetic questions which the child later formulated to herself. Answer: It must be something that needs hushing up, perhaps something dangerous.) Attempts to make the mother talk and to draw out the truth by means of artful questions were futile, so resistance meets with resistance and the introversion of love begins. Naturally the capacity for sublimation in a four-year-old child is still too meagrely developed for it to render more than symptomatic service; hence she has to rely on another compensation, that is, she resorts to one of the already abandoned infantile devices for securing love by force, preferably that of crying and calling the mother at night. This had been diligently practised and exploited during her first year. It now returns and, in keeping with her age, has become well motivated and equipped with recent impressions.

19   We should mention that the Messina earthquake had just occurred, and this event was much discussed at table. Anna was extraordinarily interested in everything to do with it, getting her grandmother to tell her over and over again how the earth shook and the houses tumbled down and how many people lost their lives. That was the beginning of her nocturnal fears; she could not be left alone, her mother had to go to her and stay with her, otherwise she was afraid that the earthquake would come and the house fall in and kill her. By day, too, she was intensely occupied with such thoughts; when out walking with her mother she would pester her with such questions as "Will the house be standing when we get home? Will Papa still be alive? Are you sure there's no earthquake at home?" At every stone in the road she would ask whether it was from the earthquake. A house under construction was a house destroyed by the

earthquake, and so on. Finally she used to cry out at night that the earthquake was coming, she could hear it rumbling. Every evening she had to be solemnly promised that no earthquake would come. Various ways of calming her were tried, for instance she was told that earthquakes only occur where there are volcanoes. But then she had to be satisfied that the mountains surrounding the town were not volcanoes. This reasoning gradually led the child to an intense and, at her age, unnatural craving for knowledge, until finally all the geological pictures and atlases had to be fetched from her father's library. For hours she would rummage through them looking for pictures of volcanoes and earthquakes, and asking endless questions.

20   We see here an energetic attempt being made to sublimate fear into a desire for knowledge, which strikes us as decidedly premature at this age. But how many gifted children, suffering from exactly the same problem, do we not see being spoon-fed on this untimely sublimation, and by no means to their advantage. For if one fosters sublimation at this age one is only strengthening a neurosis. The root of the child's desire for knowledge is fear, and the fear is the expression of converted libido, that is, of an introversion that has become neurotic and is neither necessary nor favourable to the development of the child at this age. Where this desire for knowledge is ultimately leading is made clear by a series of questions which arose almost daily: "Why is Sophie [a younger sister] younger than I? Where was Freddie [her little brother] before? Was he in heaven and what was he doing there? Why did he only come down now, why not before?"

21   Such being the state of affairs, the father decided that the mother ought to tell the child the truth about her little brother at the first favourable opportunity.

22   This presented itself when, soon afterwards, Anna again inquired about the stork. Her mother told her that the story of the stork was not true, but that Freddie grew inside his mother as the flower grows out of the earth. At first he was very little, and then he grew bigger and bigger like a plant. The child listened attentively without the least surprise and then asked:
"But did he come all by himself?"
"Yes."
"But he can't walk yet!"

17

Sophie: "Then he crawled out."

Anna (overhearing Sophie's remark): "Is there a hole here" —pointing to her chest—"or did he come out of the mouth? Who came out of the nurse?"

23   At this point she interrupted herself and exclaimed, "No, I know the stork brought him down from heaven!" Then, before the mother could answer her questions, she dropped the subject and again asked to see pictures of volcanoes. The evening following this conversation was calm. The sudden explanation had evidently produced in the child a whole chain of ideas, which announced themselves in a spate of questions. New and unexpected vistas were opened, and she rapidly approached the main problem: "Where did the baby come out? Was it from a hole in the chest or from the mouth?" Both suppositions qualify as acceptable theories. We even meet with young married women who still entertain the theory of the hole in the abdominal wall or of Caesarean section; this is supposed to betray a very unusual degree of innocence. As a matter of fact it is not innocence; in such cases we are practically always dealing with infantile sexual activities which in later life have brought the *vias naturales* into ill repute.

23a   It may be asked where the child got the absurd idea that there is a hole in the chest, or that the birth takes place through the mouth. Why did she not pick on one of the natural openings in the pelvis, from which things come out daily? The explanation is simple. It was not so very long since our little one had challenged all the educative arts of her mother by her heightened interest in both these openings and their remarkable products—an interest not always in accord with the demands of cleanliness and decorum. Then for the first time she became acquainted with the exceptional laws relating to these bodily regions and, being a sensitive child, she soon noticed that there was something taboo about them. Consequently this region had to be left out of her calculations, a trivial error of thought which may be forgiven in a child when one considers all those people who, despite the most powerful spectacles, can never see anything sexual anywhere. In this matter Anna reacted far more docilely than her little sister, whose scatological interests and achievements were certainly phenomenal and who even misbehaved in that way at table. She invariably described her excesses as "funny," but Mama said no, it was not funny, and forbade such fun. The child seemed to take these incomprehensible educational sallies in good part, but she soon had her revenge. Once when a new dish appeared on the table she categorically refused to have anything to do with it, remarking that it was "not funny." Thereafter all culinary novelties were declined on the ground that they were "not funny."

24   The psychology of this negativism is quite typical and is not hard to fathom. The logic of feeling says simply: "If you don't find my little tricks funny and make me give them up, then I won't find your tricks funny either, and won't play with you." Like all childish compensations of this kind, this works on the important infantile principle "It serves you right when I'm hurt."

25   After this digression, let us return to our theme. Anna had merely shown herself docile and had so adjusted herself to the cultural demands that she thought (or at least spoke) of the simplest things last. The incorrect theories that have been substituted for the correct ones sometimes persist for years, until brusque enlightenment comes from without. It is therefore no wonder that such theories, the formation of and adherence to which is favoured even by parents and educationists, should later become determinants of important symptoms in a neurosis, or of delusions in a psychosis, as I have shown in my "Psychology of Dementia Praecox." [6] Things that have existed in the psyche for years always remain somewhere, even though they may be hidden under compensations of a seemingly different nature.

26   But even before the question is settled as to where the child actually comes out a new problem obtrudes itself: children come out of Mama, but how about the nurse? Did someone come out of her too? Then follows the abrupt exclamation, "No, I know the stork brought him down from heaven!" What is there so peculiar about the fact that nobody came out of the nurse? We recall that Anna has identified herself with the nurse and plans to become a nurse later, for she too would like to have a child, and she could get one just as easily as the nurse had

6 *Coll. Works*, Vol. 3. [See bibliographical note at end of this volume for other sources of Jung's writings in volumes of the *Collected Works* not yet published. —Editors.]

done. But now, when it is known that little brother grew in Mama, what is to be done?

27   This disquieting question is averted by a quick return to the stork-angel theory, which had never really been believed and which after a few trials is definitely abandoned. Two questions, however, remain in the air. The first is: where does the child come out? and the second, a considerably more difficult one: how is it that Mama has children while the nurse and the servants do not? Neither question is asked for the time being.

28   The next day at lunch, Anna announced, apparently out of the blue, "My brother is in Italy and has a house made of cloth and glass and it doesn't fall down."

29   Here as always it was impossible to ask for an explanation; the resistances were too great, and Anna would not have let herself be pinned down. This unique and rather officious announcement is very significant. For some three months the children had been spinning a stereotyped fantasy of a "big brother" who knew everything, could do everything, and had everything. He had been to all the places where they had not been, was allowed to do all the things they were not allowed to do, was the owner of enormous cows, horses, sheep, dogs, etc.[7] Each of them had such a big brother. The source of this fantasy is not far to seek: its model is the father, who seems to be rather like a brother to Mama. So the children too must have an equally powerful brother. This brother is very brave, he is at present in dangerous Italy and lives in an impossibly fragile house which does not fall down. For the child this is an important wish-fulfilment: the earthquake is no longer dangerous. In consequence the fear and anxiety were banished and did not return. The fear of earthquakes now entirely disappeared. Instead of calling her father to her bedside every evening to conjure away the fear, she now became more affectionate and begged him to kiss her good night. In order to test this new state of affairs, the father showed her more pictures of volcanoes and earthquakes, but Anna remained indifferent and examined the pictures coldly: "Dead people! I've seen all that before." Even the photograph of a volcanic eruption no longer held any attractions for her. Thus all her scientific interest collapsed and vanished as sud-

7 This is a primitive definition of God.

denly as it had come. However, during the days that followed her enlightenment Anna had more important matters to attend to, for she had her newly found knowledge to disseminate among her circle of acquaintances. She began by recounting, at great length, how Freddie had grown in Mama, and herself and her younger sister likewise; how Papa grew in *his* mother and Mama in *her* mother, and the servants in their respective mothers. By dint of numerous questions she also tested whether her knowledge was firmly founded in truth, for her suspicions had been aroused in no small degree, so that repeated corroboration was needed to dissipate all her misgivings. In between times the children brought up the stork-angel theory again, but in a less believing tone, and even lectured the dolls in a singsong voice.

30   The new knowledge, however, obviously held its ground, for the phobia did not return.

31   Only once did her certainty threaten to go to pieces. About a week after the enlightenment her father had to spend the morning in bed with an attack of influenza. The children knew nothing of this, and Anna, coming into her parents' bedroom, saw the unexpected sight of her father lying in bed. She made an oddly surprised face, remained standing far away from the bed, and would not come nearer, evidently feeling shy and mistrustful again. Suddenly she burst out with the question "Why are you in bed? Have you got a plant in your inside too?"

32   Naturally her father had to laugh, and assured her that children never grew in their fathers, that as a matter of fact men did not have children, but only women, whereupon the child instantly became friendly again. But though the surface was calm the problems went on working in the depths. A few days later Anna again announced at lunch, "I had a dream last night about Noah's Ark." The father then asked her what she had dreamed, to which Anna only let out a stream of nonsense. In such cases one must simply wait and pay attention. Sure enough, after a few minutes Anna said to her grandmother, "I had a dream last night about Noah's Ark and there were lots of little animals in it." Another pause. Then she began the story for the third time: *"I had a dream last night about Noah's Ark and there were lots of little animals in it and underneath there was a lid which opened and all the little animals fell out."* Knowledge-

21

able persons will understand the fantasy. The children really did have a Noah's Ark, but the opening, a lid, was in the roof and not underneath. This is a delicate hint that the story about children being born from the mouth or chest was wrong, and that she had a pretty good idea of where they did come out— namely, from underneath.

33   Several weeks now passed without any noteworthy occurrences. There was one dream: *"I dreamt about Papa and Mama, they were sitting up late in the study and we children were there too."*

34   On the face of it this is just the well-known wish of children to be allowed to stay up as long as the parents. This wish is here realized, or rather it is used to mask a much more important wish, the wish to be present in the evenings when the parents are alone, and—naturally and innocently enough—in the *study* where she had seen all those interesting books and had satisfied her thirst for knowledge. In other words, she was really seeking an answer to the burning question of where little brother came from. If the children were there they would find out.

35   A few days later Anna had a nightmare, from which she awoke screaming, "The earthquake is coming, the house is beginning to shake!" Her mother went to her and comforted her, saying that there was no earthquake, everything was quiet and everybody was asleep. Then Anna said in an urgent tone, "I'd just like to see the spring, how all the little flowers come out and how all the fields are full of flowers; I want to see Freddie, he has such a dear little face. What is Papa doing—what did he say?" Her mother told her he was asleep and hadn't said anything. Anna then remarked, with a sarcastic smile, "He will probably be sick again in the morning!"

36   This text must be read backwards. The last sentence is not intended seriously, as it was uttered in a sarcastic tone of voice. The last time father was sick Anna suspected him of having "a plant in his inside." The sarcasm therefore means "He will probably have a child in the morning!" But this is not intended seriously, for Papa cannot have a child, only Mama has children; perhaps she will have another tomorrow, but where from? "What is Papa doing?" Here we have an unmistakable formulation of the difficult problem: what does Papa do if he does not produce children? Anna would very much like to find the clue

22

to all her problems; she would like to know how Freddie came into the world, she would like to see how the flowers come out of the earth in the spring, and these wishes all hide behind her fear of earthquakes.

37   After this intermezzo Anna slept peacefully until morning. In the morning her mother asked her what was the matter with her last night. Anna had forgotten everything and thought she had only had a dream: *"I dreamt I could make the summer and then someone threw a golliwog down the toilet."*

38   This singular dream is made up of two different scenes, which are separated by the word "then." The second part derives its material from a recent wish to have a golliwog, i.e., to have a masculine doll just as Mama has a little boy. Someone throws the golliwog down the toilet—but usually one lets quite other things drop down the toilet. The inference is that children come out just like the things into the toilet. Here we have an analogy to the *Lumpf*-theory of Little Hans. Whenever several scenes are found in one dream, each scene ordinarily represents a special variation of the working out of the complex. Thus the first part is only a variation of the theme found in the second part. We have noted above what is meant by "seeing the spring" or "seeing the flowers come out." Anna now dreams that she *can make the summer,* i.e., can cause the flowers to come out; she herself can make a little child, and the second part of the dream represents this as analogous to the making of a motion. Here we put our finger on the egoistic wish which lies behind the seemingly objective interest of the previous night's conversation.

39   A few days later the mother received a visit from a lady who was looking forward to her confinement. The children apparently noticed nothing. But the next day they amused themselves, under the guidance of the elder girl, by taking all the old newspapers out of their father's waste-paper basket and stuffing them under their frocks in front, so that the imitation was unmistakable. That night Anna again had a dream: *"I dreamt about a lady in the town, she had a very fat stomach."* As the chief actor in a dream is always the dreamer himself under a definite aspect, the game of the day before finds complete interpretation.

40   Not long after, Anna surprised her mother with the following performance: she stuck her doll under her clothes and slowly pulled it out head downwards, saying, "Look, the baby is com-

23

ing out, now it is all out." Anna was telling her mother: thus I conceive the problem of birth. What do you think of it? is it right? The game is really meant as a question, for, as we shall see later, this conception still had to be officially confirmed.

41   Rumination on the problem by no means ended here, as is apparent from the ideas Anna conceived during the following weeks. Thus she repeated the same game a few days later with her Teddy bear, which had the function of a specially beloved doll. Another day, pointing to a rose, she said to her grandmother, "Look, the rose is getting a baby." As the grandmother did not quite take her meaning, the child pointed to the swollen calyx: "Don't you see, it's all fat here!"

42   One day she was quarrelling with her younger sister, when the latter exclaimed angrily, "I'll kill you!" Whereupon Anna replied, "When I am dead you will be all alone, and then you'll have to pray to God for a live baby." And immediately the scene changed: Anna was the angel, and the younger sister had to kneel down before her and beg her to send a living child. In this way Anna became the child-giving mother.

43   Once they had oranges for supper. Anna impatiently asked for one and said, "I'll take an orange and I'll swallow it all down into my stomach, and then I shall get a baby."

44   This instantly reminds us of the fairytales in which childless women finally make themselves pregnant by swallowing fruit, fish and the like.[8] Anna was here trying to solve the problem of how children actually get into the mother. In so doing she takes up a position of inquiry which had never been formulated before so precisely. The solution follows in the form of an analogy, which is characteristic of the archaic thinking of the child. (Thinking in analogies is also found in the adult, in the stratum lying immediately below consciousness. Dreams bring the analogies to the surface, as also does dementia praecox.) In German and numerous other foreign fairytales one frequently finds such childish comparisons. Fairytales seem to be the myths of childhood and they therefore contain among other things the mythology which children weave for themselves concerning sexual processes. The poetry of fairytale, whose magic is felt even by the

8 Cf. Franz Riklin *Wishfulfillment and Symbolism in Fairy Tales* (trans. by W. A. White, Nervous and Mental Disease Monograph Series, No. 21, New York, 1921).

adult, rests not least upon the fact that some of the old theories are still alive in our unconscious. We experience a strange and mysterious feeling whenever a fragment of our remotest youth stirs into life again, not actually reaching consciousness, but merely shedding a reflection of its emotional intensity on the conscious mind.

45   The problem of how the child gets into the mother is a difficult one to solve. As the only way of getting things into the body is through the mouth, it stands to reason that the mother ate something like a fruit, which then grew inside her. But here another difficulty presents itself: one knows what comes out of the mother, but what is the use of the father? Now, it is an old rule of the mental economy to connect two unknowns and to use one to solve the other.

46   Hence the conviction rapidly fastened on the child that the father is somehow involved in the whole business, particularly in view of the fact that the problem of where children come from still leaves the question open of how they get into the mother.

47   What does the father do? This question occupied Anna to the exclusion of all else. One morning she ran into her parents' bedroom while they were still dressing, jumped into her father's bed, lay flat on her face, and flailed with her legs, crying out, "Look, is that what Papa does?" Her parents laughed and did not answer, as it only dawned on them afterwards what this performance probably signified. The analogy with the horse of Little Hans, which made such a commotion with its legs, is surprisingly close.

48   Here, with this latest achievement, the matter seemed to rest; at any rate the parents found no opportunity to make any pertinent observations. That the problem should come to a standstill at this point is not really surprising, for this is the most difficult part. The child knows nothing about sperms and nothing about coitus. There is but one possibility: the mother must eat something, for only in that way can anything get into the body. But what does the father do? The frequent comparisons with the nurse and other unmarried people were obviously to some purpose. Anna was bound to conclude that the existence of the father was in some way significant. But what on earth does he

25

do? Anna and Little Hans are agreed that it must have something to do with the legs.

49   This standstill lasted about five months, during which time no phobias or any other signs of a working through of the complex appeared. Then came the first premonition of future events. Anna's family were at that time living in a country house near a lake, where the children could bathe with their mother. As Anna was afraid to go more than knee-deep into the water, her father once took her right in with him, which led to a great outburst of crying. That evening, when going to bed, Anna said to her mother, "Papa wanted to drown me, didn't he?"

50   A few days later there was another outburst. She had continued to stand in the gardener's way until finally, for a joke, he picked her up and put her in a hole he had just dug. Anna started to cry miserably, and declared afterwards that the man had tried to bury her.

51   The upshot was that Anna woke up one night with fearful screams. Her mother went to her in the adjoining room and quieted her. Anna had dreamed that *"a train went by overhead and fell down."*

52   Here we have a parallel to the "stage coach" story of Little Hans. These incidents show clearly enough that fear was again in the air, i.e., that there was some obstacle preventing the transference of love to the parents and that therefore a large part of it was converted into fear. This time the mistrust was directed not against the mother, but against the father, who she was sure must know the secret, but would never let anything out. What could the father be doing or keeping up his sleeve? To the child this secret appeared to be something very dangerous, so obviously she felt that the worst might be expected of the father. (This childish fear of the father is to be seen particularly clearly in adults in cases of dementia praecox, which takes the lid off many unconscious processes as though it were acting on psychoanalytical principles.) Hence Anna arrived at the apparently nonsensical notion that her father wanted to drown her.

53   Meanwhile Anna had grown a little older and her interest in her father took on a special tinge which is rather hard to describe. Language has no words for the peculiar kind of tender curiosity that shone in the child's eyes.

54   It is probably no accident that the children began playing a

pretty game about this time. They called the two biggest dolls their "grandmothers" and played at hospital with them, a tool-shed being taken over as a hospital. There the grandmothers were brought, interned, and left to sit overnight. "Grandmother" in this connection is distinctly reminiscent of the "big brother" earlier. It seems very likely that the "grandmother" deputizes for the mother. So the children were already conspiring to get the mother out of the way.[9] This intention was assisted by the fact that the mother had again given Anna cause for displeasure.

55 It came about in the following way: The gardener had laid out a large bed which he was sowing with grass. Anna helped him in this work with much pleasure, apparently without guessing the profound significance of her childish play. About a fortnight later she began to observe with delight the young grass sprouting. On one of these occasions she went to her mother and asked, "How did the eyes grow into the head?"

56 Her mother told her she didn't know. But Anna went on to ask whether God knew, or her father, and why God and her father knew everything? The mother then referred her to her father, who might be able to tell her how the eyes grew into the head. Some days later there was a family gathering at tea. After the meal had broken up, the father remained at the table reading the paper, and Anna also stayed behind. Suddenly approaching her father she said, "Tell me, how did the eyes grow into the head?"

Father: "They did not grow into the head; they were there from the beginning and grew with the head."

Anna: "Weren't the eyes planted?"

Father: "No, they just grew in the head like the nose."

Anna: "But did the mouth and the ears grow like that? And the hair?"

Father: "Yes, they all grew the same way."

9 This tendency to get rid of the mother also showed itself in the following incident: The children had requisitioned the tool-shed as a house for themselves and their dolls. An important room in any house is, as we know, the toilet, which obviously cannot be lacking. Accordingly, the children went to the toilet in a corner of the tool-shed. Their mother naturally could not help spoiling this illusion by forbidding such games. Soon afterwards she caught the remark, "When Mama is dead we'll do it every day in the tool-shed and put on Sunday clothes every day."

Anna: "Even the hair? But the baby mice come into the world all naked. Where was the hair before? Aren't there little seeds for it?"

Father: "No. The hair, you see, comes out of little granules which are like seeds, but they are already in the skin and nobody sowed them there."

57 The father was now getting into a fix. He guessed where the little one was leading him, therefore he did not want to upset, on account of a single false application, the diplomatically introduced seed theory which she had most fortunately picked up from nature; for the child spoke with an unwonted earnestness which compelled consideration.

58 Anna (visibly disappointed, and in a distressed voice): "But how did Freddie get into Mama? Who stuck him in? And who stuck you into your mama? Where did he come out?"

59 From this sudden storm of questions the father chose the last for his first answer:

"Think, now, you know that Freddie is a boy; boys grow into men and girls into women, and only women can have children. Now, just think, where could Freddie have come out?"

Anna (laughing joyfully and pointing to her genitals): "Did he come out here?"

Father: "But of course. Surely you must have thought of that before?"

Anna (overlooking the question): "But how did Freddie get into Mama? Did anybody plant him? Was the seed sown?"

60 This extremely precise question could no longer be evaded by the father. He explained to the child, who listened with the greatest attention, that the mother is like the soil and the father like the gardener; that the father provides the seed which grows in the mother and thus produces a baby. This answer gave her extraordinary satisfaction; she immediately ran to her mother and said, "Papa has told me everything, now I know it all." But what it was she knew, she never told to anyone.

61 The new knowledge was, however, put into practice the following day. Anna went up to her mother and said brightly: "Just think, Mama, Papa told me that Freddie was a little angel and was brought down from heaven by the stork." Her mother was naturally astounded, and said, "I am quite certain your

28

father never told you anything of the sort." Whereupon the little one skipped away laughing.

62   This was her revenge. Her mother evidently would not or could not tell her how the eyes grew into the head; she didn't even know how Freddie had got into her. Therefore she could easily be led up the garden path with that old story about the stork. She might believe it still.

* * *

63   The child was now satisfied, for her knowledge had been enriched and a difficult problem solved. An even greater advantage, however, was the fact that she had won a more intimate relationship with her father, which did not prejudice her intellectual independence in the least. The father of course was left with an uneasy feeling, for he was not altogether happy about having passed on to a four-and-a-half-year-old child a secret which other parents carefully guard. He was disquieted by the thought of what Anna might do with her knowledge. What if she was indiscreet and exploited it? She might so easily instruct her playmates or gleefully play the *enfant terrible* with grown-ups. But these fears proved to be groundless. Anna never breathed a word about it, either then or at any time. The enlightenment had, moreover, brought a complete silencing of the problem, so that no more questions presented themselves. Yet the unconscious did not lose sight of the riddle of human creation. A few weeks after her enlightenment Anna recounted the following dream: She was *"in the garden and several gardeners stood making wee-wee against the trees, and Papa was also doing it."*

64   This recalls the earlier unsolved problem: what does the father do?

65   Also about this time a carpenter came into the house in order to repair an ill-fitting cupboard; Anna stood by and watched him planing the wood. That night she dreamt that the carpenter "sliced off" her genitals.

66   The dream could be interpreted to mean that Anna was asking herself: will it work with me? oughtn't one to do something like what the carpenter did, in order to make it work? Such an hypothesis would indicate that this problem is particularly active in the unconscious at the moment, because there is

29

something not quite clear about it. That this is so was shown by the next incident, which did not, however, occur until several months later, when Anna was approaching her fifth birthday. Meantime the younger sister, Sophie, was taking a growing interest in these matters. She had been present when Anna received enlightenment at the time of the earthquake phobia, and had even thrown in an apparently understanding remark on that occasion, as the reader may remember. But in actual fact the explanation was not understood by her at the time. This became clear soon afterwards. She had days when she was more than usually affectionate with her mother and never left her skirts; but she could also be really naughty and irritable. On one of these bad days she tried to tip her little brother out of the pram. Her mother scolded her, whereupon she set up a loud wailing. Suddenly, in the midst of her tears, she said, "I don't know anything about where children come from!" She was then given the same explanation that her elder sister had received earlier. This seemed to allay the problem for her, and for several months there was peace. Then once more there were days when she was whining and bad-tempered. One day, quite out of the blue, she turned to her mother with the question "Was Freddie really in your inside?"

Mother: "Yes."

Sophie: "Did you push him out?"

Mother: "Yes."

Anna (butting in): "But was it down below?"

67   Here Anna employed a childish term which is used for the genitals as well as for the anus.

Sophie: "And then you let him drop down?"

68   The expression "drop down" comes from that toilet mechanism, of such absorbing interest to children, whereby one lets the excreta drop down into the bowl.

Anna: "Or was he sicked up?"

69   The evening before, Anna had been sick owing to a slightly upset stomach.

70   After a pause of several months Sophie had suddenly caught up and now wished to make sure of the explanation previously vouchsafed to her. This making doubly sure seems to indicate that doubts had arisen concerning the explanation given by her mother. To judge by the content of the questions, the doubts

arose because the process of birth had not been adequately explained. "Push" is a word children sometimes use for the act of defecation. It tells us along what lines the theory will develop with Sophie, too. Her further remark, as to whether one had let Freddie "drop down," betrays such a complete identification of her baby brother with excrement that it borders on the ludicrous. To this Anna makes the singular remark that perhaps Freddie was "sicked up." Her own vomiting of the day before had made a deep impression on her. It was the first time she had been sick since her earliest childhood. That was one way in which things could leave the body, though she had obviously not given it serious thought until now. (Only once had it occurred to her, and that was when they were discussing the body openings and she had thought of the mouth.) Her remark is a firm pointer away from the excrement theory. Why did she not point at once to the genitals? Her last dream gives us a clue to the probable reasons: there is something about the genitals which Anna still does not understand; something or other has to be done there to make it "work." Maybe it wasn't the genitals at all; maybe the seed for little children got into the body through the mouth, like food, and the child came out like "sick."

71   The detailed mechanism of birth, therefore, was still puzzling. Anna was again told by her mother that the child really does come out down below. About a month later, Anna suddenly had the following dream: *"I dreamt I was in the bedroom of Uncle and Auntie. Both of them were in bed. I pulled the bedclothes off Uncle, lay on his stomach, and joggled up and down on it."*

72   This dream came like a bolt from the blue. The children were then on holiday for several weeks and the father, who had been detained in town on business, had arrived on that same day for a visit. Anna was especially affectionate with him. He asked her jokingly, "Will you travel up to town with me this evening?" Anna: "Yes, and then I can sleep with you?" All this time she hung lovingly on her father's arm as her mother sometimes did. A few moments later she brought out her dream. Some days previously she had been staying as a guest with the aunt mentioned in the dream (the dream, too, was some days old). She had looked forward particularly to that visit, because

she was certain she would meet two small cousins—boys—in whom she showed an unfeigned interest. Unfortunately, the cousins were not there, and Anna was very disappointed. There must have been something in her present situation that was related to the content of the dream for it to be remembered so suddenly. The relation between the manifest content and the conversation with her father is clear enough. The uncle was a decrepit old gentleman and only known to the child from a few rare encounters. In the dream he is patently a substitute for her father. The dream itself creates a substitute for the disappointment of the day before: she is in bed with her father. Here we have the *tertium comparationis* with the present. Hence the sudden remembrance of the dream. The dream recapitulates a game which Anna often played in her father's (empty) bed, the game of joggling about and kicking with her legs on the mattress. From this game stemmed the question "Is this what Papa does?" Her immediate disappointment is that her father answered her question with the words, "You can sleep by yourself in the next room." Then follows the remembrance of the same dream which has already consoled her for a previous erotic disappointment (with the cousins). At the same time the dream is essentially an illustration of the theory that "it" takes place in bed, and by means of the aforementioned rhythmical movements. Whether the remark that she lay on her uncle's stomach had anything to do with her being sick cannot be proved.

73   Such is the extent of our observations up to the present. Anna is now a little over five years old and already in possession, as we have seen, of a number of the most important sexual facts. Any adverse effect of this knowledge upon her morals and character has yet to be observed. Of the favourable therapeutic effect we have spoken already. It is also quite clear from the report that the younger sister is in need of a special explanation for herself, as and when the problem arises for her. If the time is not ripe, no amount of enlightenment, it would seem, is of the slightest use.

74   I am no apostle of sex education for schoolchildren, or indeed of any standardized mechanical explanations. I am therefore not in a position to offer any positive and uniformly valid advice. I can only draw one conclusion from the material here recorded, which is, that we should try to see children as they

really are, and not as we would wish them; that, in educating them, we should follow the natural path of development, and eschew dead prescriptions.

Supplement

75 As already mentioned in the foreword, our views have undergone a considerable change since this paper was first published. There is, in the observations, one point in particular which has not been sufficiently appreciated, namely the fact that again and again, despite the enlightenment they received, the children exhibited a distinct preference for some fantastic explanation. Since the first appearance of the present work this tendency, contrary to my expectations, has increased: the children continue to favour a fantastic theory. In this matter I have before me a number of incontestable observations, some of them concerning the children of other parents. The four-year-old daughter of one of my friends, for instance, who does not hold with useless secrecy in education, was allowed last year to help her mother decorate the Christmas tree. But this year the child told her mother, "It wasn't right last year. This time I'll not look and you will lock the door with the key."

76 As a result of this and similar observations, I have been left wondering whether the fantastic or mythological explanation preferred by the child might not, for that very reason, be more suitable than a "scientific" one, which, although factually correct, threatens to clamp down the latch on fantasy for good. In the present instance the latch could be unclamped again, but only because the fantasy brushed "science" aside.

77 Did their enlightenment harm the children? Nothing of the sort was observed. They developed healthily and normally. The problems they broached apparently sank right into the background, presumably as a result of the manifold external interests arising out of school life, and the like. The fantasy activity was not harmed in the least, nor did it pursue paths that could be described as in any way abnormal. Occasional remarks or observations of a delicate nature were made openly and without secrecy.

78 I have therefore come to hold the view that the earlier free

discussions took the wind out of the children's imagination and thus prevented any secretive fantasy from developing which would have cast a sidelong glance at these things, and would, in consequence, have been nothing but an obstacle to the free development of thinking. The fact that the fantasy activity simply ignored the right explanation seems, in my view, to be an important indication that all freely developing thought has an irresistible need to emancipate itself from the realism of fact and to create a world of its own.

79   Consequently, however little advisable it is to give children false explanations which would only sow the seeds of mistrust, it is, so it seems to me, no less inadvisable to insist on the acceptance of the right explanation. For the freedom of the mind's development would merely be suppressed through such rigid consistency, and the child forced into a concretism of outlook that would preclude further development. Side by side with the biological, the spiritual, too, has its inviolable rights. It is assuredly no accident that primitive peoples, even in adult life, make the most fantastic assertions about well-known sexual processes, as for instance that coitus has nothing to do with pregnancy.[10] From this it has been concluded that these people do not even know there is such a connection. But more accurate investigation has shown that they know very well that with animals copulation is followed by pregnancy. Only for human beings is it denied—not *not known,* but flatly *denied*—that this is so, for the simple reason that they prefer a mythological explanation which has freed itself from the trammels of concretism. It is not hard to see that in these facts, so frequently observed among primitives, there lie the beginnings of *abstraction,* which is so very important for culture. We have every reason to suppose that this is also true of the psychology of the child. If certain South American Indians really and truly call themselves red cockatoos and expressly repudiate a figurative interpretation of this fact, this has absolutely nothing to do with any sexual repression on "moral" grounds, but is due to the law of independence inherent in the thinking function and to its emancipation from the concretism of sensuous perceptions. We

10 [Cf. Bronislaw Malinowski, *The Sexual Life of Savages* (3rd edn., London and New York, 1932).—Editors.]

must assign a separate principle to the thinking function, a principle which coincides with the beginnings of sexuality only in the polyvalent germinal disposition of the very young child. To reduce the origins of thinking to mere sexuality is an undertaking that runs counter to the basic facts of human psychology.

II

INTRODUCTION TO WICKES'S
"ANALYSE DER KINDERSEELE"

INTRODUCTION TO WICKES'S
"ANALYSE DER KINDERSEELE" [1]

80   What this book provides is not theory, but experience. That is just what gives it its special value for anyone really interested in child psychology. We cannot fully understand the psychology of the child or that of the adult if we regard it as the subjective concern of the individual alone, for almost more important than this is his relation to others. Here, at all events, we can begin with the most easily accessible and, practically speaking, the most important part of the psychic life of the child. Children are so deeply involved in the psychological attitude of their parents that it is no wonder that most of the nervous disturbances in childhood can be traced back to a disturbed psychic atmosphere in the home. This book shows, from a series of remarkable examples, just how disastrous the parental influence can be for the child. Probably no father or mother will be able

---

[1] [The first three and a half paragraphs originally appeared as an introduction to Frances G. Wickes, *The Inner World of Childhood* (New York, 1927). The book was subsequently translated into German as *Analyse der Kinderseele* (Stuttgart, 1931), and for it Professor Jung expanded his introduction to the present dimensions. It is here translated entirely anew.

Mrs. Wickes worked for many years as a psychologist in schools. She collected numerous case studies, and these were later illuminated for her when she encountered Professor Jung's theories, which she was able to confirm and extend. The most important part of her thesis demonstrates how the unconscious of parents can cause many psychic disorders of childhood.—EDITORS.]

39

to read these chapters without realizing the devastating truths of this book. *Exempla docent*—example is the best teacher! Once more this proves to be a well-worn yet pitiless truth. It is not a question of good and wise counsels, but solely of deeds, of the actual life of the parents. Nor is it a matter of living in accordance with accepted moral values, for the observance of customs and laws can very easily be a cloak for a lie so subtle that our fellow human beings are unable to detect it. It may help us to escape all criticism, we may even be able to deceive ourselves in the belief of our obvious righteousness. But deep down, below the surface of the average man's conscience, he hears a voice whispering, "There is something not right," no matter how much his rightness is supported by public opinion or by the moral code. Certain instances in this book show very clearly that there exists a terrible law which stands beyond man's morality and his ideas of rightness—a law which cannot be cheated.

81   Besides the problem of environmental influence, the book also gives due weight to psychic factors which have more to do with the irrational values of the child than with his rational psychology. The latter can be made the object of scientific research, while the spiritual values, the qualities of the soul, elude purely intellectual treatment. It is no good having sceptical ideas about this—nature does not care a pin for our ideas. If we have to deal with the human soul we can only meet it on its own ground, and we are bound to do so whenever we are confronted with the real and crushing problems of life.

82   I am glad the author has not shrunk from opening the door to intellectual criticism. Genuine experience has nothing to fear from objections, whether justified or unjustified, for it always holds the stronger position.

83   Although this book does not pretend to be "scientific," it is scientific in a higher sense, because it gives a true picture of the difficulties that actually occur in the upbringing of children. It merits the serious attention of everybody who has anything to do with children, either by vocation or from duty. But it will also be of interest to those who, neither for reasons of duty nor from educational inclination, wish to know more about the beginnings of human consciousness. Even though many of the views and experiences set forth in this book have nothing fundamentally new to offer to the doctor and psychological educator,

the curious reader will now and then come upon cases which are strange and will give pause to his critical understanding— cases and facts which the author, with her essentially practical turn of mind, does not pursue in all their complexities and theoretical implications. What is the thoughtful reader to make, for instance, of the puzzling but undeniable fact of the identity of the psychic state of the child with the unconscious of the parents? One is dimly aware here of a region full of incalculable possibilities, a hydra-headed monster of a problem that is as much the concern of the biologist and psychologist as of the philosopher. For anyone acquainted with the psychology of primitives there is an obvious connection between this "iden- tity" and Lévy-Bruhl's idea of "participation mystique." Strange to say, there are not a few ethnologists who still kick against this brilliant idea, for which the unfortunate expression "mystique" may have to shoulder no small part of the blame. The word "mystical" has indeed become the abode of all unclean spirits, although it was not meant like that originally, but has been debased by sordid usage. There is nothing "mystical" about identity, any more than there is anything mystical about the metabolism common to mother and embryo. Identity derives essentially from the notorious unconsciousness of the small child. Therein lies the connection with the primitive, for the primitive is as unconscious as a child. Unconsciousness means non-differentiation. There is as yet no clearly differentiated ego, only events which may belong to me or to another. It is sufficient that *somebody* should be affected by them. The extraordinary infectiousness of emotional reactions then makes it certain that everybody in the vicinity will involuntarily be affected. The weaker ego-consciousness is, the less it matters who is affected, and the less the individual is able to guard against it. He could only do that if he could say: you are excited or angry, but I am not, for I am not you. The child is in exactly the same position in the family: he is affected to the same degree and in the same way as the whole group.

84   For all lovers of theory, the essential fact behind all this is that the things which have the most powerful effect upon children do not come from the conscious state of the par- ents but from their unconscious background. For the ethi- cally minded person who may be a father or mother this

presents an almost frightening problem, because the things we can manipulate more or less, namely consciousness and its contents, are seen to be ineffectual in comparison with these uncontrollable effects in the background, no matter how hard we may try. One is afflicted with a feeling of extreme moral uncertainty when one takes these unconscious processes with the seriousness they deserve. How are we to protect our children from ourselves, if conscious will and conscious effort are of no avail? There can be no doubt that it is of the utmost value for parents to view their children's symptoms in the light of their own problems and conflicts. It is their duty as parents to do so. Their responsibility in this respect carries with it the obligation to do everything in their power not to lead a life that could harm the children. Generally far too little stress is laid upon how important the conduct of the parents is for the child, because it is not words that count, but deeds. Parents should always be conscious of the fact that they themselves are the principal cause of neurosis in their children.

85   We must not, however, exaggerate the importance of unconscious effects, even though the mind's love of causes finds dangerous satisfaction in doing precisely this. Nor should we exaggerate the importance of causality in general. Certainly causes exist, but the psyche is not a mechanism that reacts of necessity and in a regular way to a specific stimulus. Here as elsewhere in practical psychology we are constantly coming up against the experience that in a family of several children only one of them will react to the unconscious of the parents with a marked degree of identity, while the others show no such reaction. The specific constitution of the individual plays a part here that is practically decisive. For this reason, the biologically trained psychologist seizes upon the fact of organic heredity and is far more inclined to regard the whole mass of genealogical inheritance as the elucidating factor, rather than the psychic causality of the moment. This standpoint, however satisfying it may be by and large, is unfortunately of little relevance to individual cases because it offers no practical clue to psychological treatment. For it also happens to be true that psychic causality exists between parents and children regardless of all the laws of heredity; in fact, the heredity point of view, although undoubtedly justified, diverts the interest of the educator or thera-

pist away from the practical importance of parental influence to some generalized and more or less fatalistic regard for the dead hand of heredity, from the consequences of which there is no escape.

86   It would be a very grave omission for parents and educators to ignore psychic causality, just as it would be a fatal mistake to attribute all the blame to this factor alone. In every case both factors have a part to play, without the one excluding the other.

87   What usually has the strongest psychic effect on the child is the life which the parents (and ancestors too, for we are dealing here with the age-old psychological phenomenon of original sin) have not lived. This statement would be rather too perfunctory and superficial if we did not add by way of qualification: that part of their lives which *might have been* lived had not certain somewhat threadbare excuses prevented the parents from doing so. To put it bluntly, it is that part of life which they have always shirked, probably by means of a pious lie. That sows the most virulent germs.

88   Our author's exhortation to clear-eyed self-knowledge is therefore altogether appropriate. The nature of the case must then decide how much of the blame really rests with the parents. One should never forget that it is a question of "original sin," a sin against life and not a contravention of man-made morality, and that the parents must therefore be viewed as children of the grandparents. The curse of the House of Atreus is no empty phrase.

89   Nor should one fall into the error of thinking that the form or intensity of the child's reaction necessarily depends upon the peculiar nature of the parent's problems. Very often these act as a catalyst and produce effects which could be better explained by heredity than by psychic causality.

90   The causal significance of parental problems for the psyche of the child would be seriously misunderstood if they were always interpreted in an exaggeratedly personal way as moral problems. More often we seem to be dealing with some fate-like ethos beyond the reach of our conscious judgment. Such things as proletarian inclinations in the scions of noble families, outbursts of criminality in the offspring of the respectable or overvirtuous, a paralysing or impassioned laziness in the children of successful business men, are not just bits of life that have been

left deliberately unlived, but compensations wrought by fate, functions of a natural ethos which casts down the high and mighty and exalts the humble. Against this neither education nor psychotherapy is of any avail. The most they can do, if reasonably applied, is to encourage the child to fulfil the task imposed upon him by the natural ethos. The guilt of the parents is impersonal, and the child should pay for it no less impersonally.

91   Parental influence only becomes a moral problem in face of conditions which might have been changed by the parents, but were not, either from gross negligence, slothfulness, neurotic anxiety, or soulless conventionality. In this matter a grave responsibility often rests with the parents. And nature has no use for the plea that one "did not know."

92   Not knowing acts like guilt.

93   Frances Wickes's book also raises the following problem in the mind of the thoughtful reader:

The psychology of "identity," which precedes ego-consciousness, indicates what the child is by virtue of his parents. But what he is as an individuality distinct from his parents can hardly be explained by the causal relationship to the parents. We ought rather to say that it is not so much the parents as their ancestors—the grandparents and great-grandparents—who are the true progenitors, and that these explain the individuality of the children far more than the immediate and, so to speak, accidental parents. In the same way the true psychic individuality of the child is something new in respect of the parents and cannot be derived from their psyche. It is a combination of collective factors which are only potentially present in the parental psyche, and are sometimes wholly invisible. Not only the child's body, but his soul, too, proceeds from his ancestry, in so far as it is individually distinct from the collective psyche of mankind.

94   The child's psyche, prior to the stage of ego-consciousness, is very far from being empty and devoid of content. Scarcely has speech developed when, in next to no time, consciousness is present; and this, with its momentary contents and its memories, exercises an intensive check upon the previous collective contents. That such contents exist in the child who has not yet attained to ego-consciousness is a well-attested fact. The most important evidence in this respect is the dreams of three- and

four-year-old children, among which there are some so strik-ingly mythological and so fraught with meaning that one would take them at once for the dreams of grown-ups, did one not know who the dreamer was. They are the last vestiges of a dwindling collective psyche which dreamingly reiterates the perennial contents of the human soul. From this phase there spring many childish fears and dim, unchildlike premonitions which, rediscovered in later phases of life, form the basis of the belief in reincarnation. But from this sphere also spring those flashes of insight and lucidity which give rise to the proverb: Children and fools speak the truth.

95 Because of its universal distribution the collective psyche, which is still so close to the small child, perceives not only the background of the parents, but, ranging further afield, the depths of good and evil in the human soul. The unconscious psyche of the child is truly limitless in extent and of incalculable age. Behind the longing to be a child again, or behind the anxiety dreams of children, there is, with all due respect to the parents, more than the joys of the cradle or a bad upbringing.

96 Primitive peoples often hold the belief that the soul of the child is the incarnation of an ancestral spirit, for which reason it is dangerous to punish children, lest the ancestral spirit be provoked. This belief is only a more concrete formulation of the views I have outlined above.

97 The infinity of the child's preconscious soul may disappear with it, or it may be preserved. The remnants of the child-soul in the adult are his best and worst qualities; at all events they are the mysterious *spiritus rector* of our weightiest deeds and of our individual destinies, whether we are conscious of it or not. It is they which make kings or pawns of the insignificant figures who move about on the checker-board of life, turning some poor devil of a casual father into a ferocious tyrant, or a silly goose of an unwilling mother into a goddess of fate. For behind every individual father there stands the primordial image of the Father, and behind the fleeting personal mother the magical figure of the Magna Mater. These archetypes of the collective psyche, whose power is magnified in immortal works of art and in the fiery tenets of religion, are the dominants that rule the preconscious soul of the child and, when projected upon the human parents, lend them a fascination which often

assumes monstrous proportions. From that there arises the false aetiology of neurosis which, in Freud, ossified into a system: the Oedipus complex. And that is also why, in the later life of the neurotic, the images of the parents can be criticized, corrected, and reduced to human dimensions, while yet continuing to work like divine agencies. Did the human father really possess this mysterious power, his sons would soon liquidate him or, even better, would refrain from becoming fathers themselves. For what ethical person could possibly bear so gigantic a responsibility? Far better to leave this sovereign power to the gods, with whom it had always rested before man became "enlightened."

III

CHILD DEVELOPMENT AND EDUCATION

CHILD DEVELOPMENT AND EDUCATION [1]

98   It is with a certain hesitation that I undertake the task of presenting to you, in a brief lecture, the connection between the findings of analytical psychology and the general problems of education. In the first place, it is a large and extensive field of human experience which cannot possibly be covered in a few pithy sentences. Furthermore, analytical psychology deals with a method and a system of thought neither of which can be assumed to be generally known. Hence their applicability to educational problems is not easily demonstrated. An historical introduction to the way in which this youngest of the psychological sciences has developed is almost indispensable, for it enables us to understand many things which, if we met them today for the first time, would be most difficult to grasp.

99   Developing out of therapeutic experiences with hypnotism, psychoanalysis, as Freud termed it, became a specific medical technique for investigating the causes of functional, or non-organic, nervous disorders. It was primarily concerned with the sexual origins of these disorders, and its value as a method of therapy was based on the assumption that a permanent curative

1 [This lecture was delivered at the International Congress of Education, in Territet (near Montreux) in 1923, and was published in *Contributions to Analytical Psychology* (London and New York, 1928) as the first of four lectures on "Analytical Psychology and Education," the others being those which follow in the present volume. It was never published in German, but a translation of the original manuscript was made for that volume by H. G. and C. F. Baynes. The present text has been somewhat revised by the author, but is in the main identical with the Baynes version, upon which it is based.—EDITORS.]

49

effect would result from bringing the sexual causes to consciousness. The entire Freudian school still takes this view of psychoanalysis and refuses to recognize any causation of nervous disorders other than the sexual. Although originally subscribing to this method, I have, during the course of years, developed the conception of *analytical psychology,* which lays stress on the fact that psychological investigation along psychoanalytic lines has left the narrow confines of a medical technique, with its restriction to certain theoretical assumptions, and has passed over into the general field of normal psychology. Therefore, when I speak of the connection between analytical psychology and education, I am leaving Freudian analysis out of account. Since the latter is a psychology which deals exclusively with the ramifications of the sexual instinct in the psyche, it would be pertinent to the discussion only if we were dealing exclusively with the sexual psychology of the child. But at the outset I must make it perfectly clear that I in no way support those views which maintain that the relation of the child to the parents, or to his brothers, sisters, comrades, is to be explained simply as the immature beginnings of the sexual function. Those views, surely not unknown to you, are in my opinion premature and one-sided generalizations which have already given rise to the most absurd misinterpretations. When pathological phenomena are present to a degree which would justify a psychological explanation along sexual lines, it is not the child's own psychology that is fundamentally responsible, but the sexually disturbed psychology of the parents. The mind of the child is extremely susceptible and dependent, and is steeped for a long time in the atmosphere of his parental psychology, only freeing itself from this influence relatively late, if at all.[2]

100   I will now try to give you some idea of the fundamental viewpoints of analytical psychology which are useful in considering the mind of the child, especially at school age. You must not think that I am in a position to offer you a list of hints for immediate application. All I can do is to provide a deeper insight into the general laws which underlie the psychic development of the child. But I shall be content if, from what I am able to give

2 [Professor Jung's position with regard to infantile sexuality is made clear in the first paper in this volume, "Psychic Conflicts in a Child," and elsewhere in his writings.—Editors.]

you, you carry away a sense of the mysterious evolution of the highest human faculties. The great responsibility which devolves upon you as educators of the next generation will prevent you from forming hasty conclusions; for there are certain viewpoints which need to germinate, often for a long time, before they can profitably be put into practice. The deepened psychological knowledge of the teacher should not, as unfortunately sometimes happens, be unloaded directly on the child; rather it should help the teacher to adopt an understanding attitude towards the child's psychic life. This knowledge is definitely for adults, not for children. What *they* are given must always be something elementary, and suited to the immature mind.

101   One of the most important achievements of analytical psychology is undoubtedly the recognition of the biological structure of the mind, but it is not easy to put into a few words something that has taken many years to discover. Therefore if at first I seem to range rather far afield, I do so only in order to bring certain general reflections to bear upon the particular problem of the child-mind.

102   Experimental psychology, represented at its best by the school of Wundt, has, as you know, occupied itself exclusively with the psychology of normal consciousness, as though the mind consisted solely of conscious phenomena. But medical psychology, especially the French school, was soon forced to recognize the existence of unconscious psychic phenomena. We know today that the conscious mind consists only of those ideational complexes which are directly associated with the ego. Those psychic factors which possess only a slight degree of intensity, or those which once had intensity but have lost it again, are "under the threshold," that is, they are subliminal, and belong to the sphere of the unconscious. By virtue of its indefinite extension the unconscious might be compared to the sea, while consciousness is like an island rising out of its midst. This comparison, however, must not be pushed too far; for the relation of conscious to unconscious is essentially different from that of an island to the sea. It is not in any sense a stable relationship, but a ceaseless welling-up, a constant shifting of content; for, like the conscious, the unconscious is never at rest, never stagnant. It lives and works in a state of perpetual interaction with the conscious. Conscious contents that have lost their intensity,

or their actuality, sink into the unconscious, and this we call forgetting. Conversely, out of the unconscious, there rise up new ideas and tendencies which, as they emerge into consciousness, are known to us as fantasies and impulses. The unconscious is the matrix out of which consciousness grows; for consciousness does not enter the world as a finished product, but is the end-result of small beginnings.

103   This development takes place in the child. During the first years of life there is hardly any consciousness, though the existence of psychic processes manifests itself at a very early stage. These processes, however, are not grouped round an organized ego; they have no centre and therefore no continuity, lacking which a conscious personality is impossible. Consequently the child has in our sense no memory, despite the plasticity and susceptibility of its psychic organ. Only when the child begins to say "I" is there any perceptible continuity of consciousness. But in between there are frequent periods of unconsciousness. One can actually see the conscious mind coming into existence through the gradual unification of fragments. This process continues throughout life, but from puberty onwards it becomes slower, and fewer and fewer fragments of the unconscious are added to consciousness. The greatest and most extensive development takes place during the period between birth and the end of psychic puberty, a period that may normally extend, for a man of our climate and race, to the twenty-fifth year. In the case of a woman it usually ends when she is about nineteen or twenty. This development establishes a firm connection between the ego and the previously unconscious psychic processes, thus separating them from their source in the unconscious. In this way the conscious rises out of the unconscious like an island newly risen from the sea. We reinforce this process in children by education and culture. School is in fact a means of strengthening in a purposeful way the integration of consciousness.

104   Now if we were to ask what would happen if there were no schools, and children were left entirely to themselves, we should have to answer that they would remain largely unconscious. What kind of a state would this be? It would be a primitive state, and when such children came of age they would, despite their native intelligence, still remain primitive—savages, in fact, rather like a tribe of intelligent Negroes or Bushmen. They

would not necessarily be stupid, but merely intelligent by instinct. They would be ignorant, and therefore unconscious of themselves and the world. Beginning life on a very much lower cultural level, they would differentiate themselves only slightly from the primitive races. This possibility of regression to the primitive stage is explained by the fundamental biogenetic law which holds good not only for the development of the body, but also in all probability for that of the psyche.

105   According to this law the evolution of the species repeats itself in the embryonic development of the individual. Thus, to a certain degree, man in his embryonic life passes through the anatomical forms of primeval times. If the same law holds for the mental development of mankind, it follows that the child develops out of an originally unconscious, animal condition into consciousness, primitive at first, and then slowly becoming more civilized.

106   The condition during the first two or three years of his life, when the child is unconscious of himself, may be compared to the animal state. Just as the child in embryo is practically nothing but a part of the mother's body, and wholly dependent on her, so in early infancy the psyche is to a large extent part of the maternal psyche, and will soon become part of the paternal psyche as well. The prime psychological condition is one of fusion with the psychology of the parents, an individual psychology being only potentially present. Hence it is that the nervous and psychic disorders of children right up to school age depend very largely on disturbances in the psychic world of the parents. All parental difficulties reflect themselves without fail in the psyche of the child, sometimes with pathological results. The dreams of small children often refer more to the parents than to the child itself. Long ago I observed some very curious dreams in early childhood, for instance the first dreams patients could remember. They were "big dreams," and their content was often so very unchildlike that at first I was convinced they could be explained by the psychology of the parents. There was the case of a boy who dreamt out the whole erotic and religious problem of his father. The father could remember no dreams at all, so for some time I analysed the father through the dreams of his eight-year-old son. Eventually the father began to dream himself, and the dreams of the child stopped. Later on I realized

53

that the peculiar dreams of small children are genuine enough, since they contain archetypes which are the cause of their apparently adult character.[3]

107   A marked change occurs when the child develops consciousness of his ego, a fact which is registered by his referring to himself as "I." This change normally takes place between the third and fifth year, but it may begin earlier. From this moment we can speak of the existence of an individual psyche, though normally the psyche attains relative independence only after puberty. Up till then it has been largely the plaything of instinct and environment. The child who enters school at six is still for the most part the psychic product of his parents, endowed, it is true, with the nucleus of ego-consciousness, but incapable of asserting his unconscious individuality. One is often tempted to interpret children who are peculiar, obstinate, disobedient, or difficult to handle as especially individual or self-willed. This is a mistake. In such cases we should always examine the parental milieu, its psychological conditions and history.[4] Almost without exception we discover in the parents the only valid reasons for the child's difficulties. His disquieting peculiarities are far less the expression of his own inner life than a reflection of disturbing influences in the home. If the physician has to deal with nervous disorders in a child of this age, he will have to pay serious attention to the psychic state of the parents; to their problems, the way they live and do not live, the aspirations they have fulfilled or neglected, and to the predominant family atmosphere and the method of education. All these psychic conditions influence a child profoundly. In his early years the child lives in a state of *participation mystique* with his parents. Time and again it can be seen how he reacts immediately to any im-

3 [Attempts to persuade Professor Jung to write further about his collection of children's dreams have proved unavailing, owing to the pressure upon him of other work. He delivered, however, four series of seminars on the subject between 1935 and 1940, at the Eidgenössische Technische Hochschule, Zurich. The last three were reported by members of the seminars and the transcripts have been privately circulated. Only the third series (winter term, 1938–39) has been translated into English, likewise for private circulation.—EDITORS.]

4 I have given elsewhere a number of examples of the extraordinary kinship which exists in the psychological *habitus* of members of the same family, amounting in one case almost to identity. See "The Association Method," in *Coll. Works*, Vol. 2, part ii.

portant developments in the parental psyche. Needless to say both the parents and the child are unconscious of what is going on. The infectious nature of the parents' complexes can be seen from the effect their mannerisms have on their children. Even when they make completely successful efforts to control themselves, so that no adult could detect the least trace of a complex, the children will get wind of it somehow. I remember a very revealing case of three girls who had a *most* devoted mother. When they were approaching puberty they confessed shamefacedly to each other that for years they had suffered from horrible dreams about her. They dreamt of her as a witch or a dangerous animal, and they could not understand it at all, since their mother was so lovely and so utterly devoted to them. Years later the mother became insane, and in her insanity would exhibit a sort of lycanthropy in which she crawled about on all fours and imitated the grunting of pigs, the barking of dogs, and the growling of bears.

107a   This is an expression of primitive identity, from which the individual consciousness frees itself only gradually. In this battle for freedom the school plays a not unimportant part, as it is the first milieu the child finds outside his home. School comrades take the place of brothers and sisters; the teacher, if a man, acts as a substitute for the father, and, if a woman, for the mother. It is important that the teacher should be conscious of the role he is playing. He must not be satisfied with merely pounding the curriculum into the child; he must also influence him through his personality. This latter function is at least as important as the actual teaching, if not more so in certain cases. Though it is a misfortune for a child to have no parents, it is equally dangerous for him to be too closely bound to his family. An excessively strong attachment to the parents is a severe handicap in his later adaptation to the world, for a growing human being is not destined to remain forever the child of his parents. There are, unfortunately, many parents who keep their children infantile because they themselves do not wish to grow old and give up their parental authority and power. In this way they exercise an extremely bad influence over their children, since they deprive them of every opportunity for individual responsibility. These disastrous methods of upbringing result either in dependent personalities, or in men and women who can achieve their independence only by furtive means. There are other parents, again, who on account of their own weaknesses are not in a position to meet the child with the authority it needs if it is to take its proper place in the world. The teacher, as a personality, is then faced with the delicate task of avoiding repressive authority, while at the same time exercising that just degree of authority which is appropriate to the adult in his dealings with children. This attitude cannot be produced artificially; it can only come about in a natural way when the teacher does his duty as a man and a citizen. He must be an upright and healthy man himself, for good example still remains the best pedagogic method. But it is also true that the very best method avails nothing if its practitioner does not hold his position on his personal merits. It would be different if the only thing that mattered in school life were the methodical teaching of the curriculum. But that is at most only half the meaning of school. The other half is the real psychological education made possible through the personality of the teacher. This education means guiding the child into the larger world and widening the scope of parental training. For however careful the latter is, it can never avoid a certain one-sidedness, as the milieu always remains the same. School, on the other hand, is the first impact of the greater world which the child has to meet, and it ought to help him to free himself progressively from the parental environment. The child naturally brings to the teacher the kind of adaptation he has learned from his father; he projects the father-image upon him, with the added tendency to assimilate the personality of the teacher to the father-image. It is therefore necessary for the teacher to adopt the personal approach, or at any rate to leave the door open for such a contact. If the personal relationship of child to teacher is a good one, it matters very little whether the method of teaching is the most up to date. Success does not depend on the method, any more than it is the exclusive aim of school life to stuff the children's heads with knowledge, but rather to make them real men and women. We need not concern ourselves so much with the amount of specific information a child takes away with him from school; the thing of vital importance is that the school should succeed in freeing the young man from unconscious identity with his family, and should make him properly conscious of himself. Without this consciousness he will never know what he really wants, but will always remain dependent and imitative, with the feeling of being misunderstood and suppressed.

108   In what I have just said I have tried to give you a general picture of the child psyche from the standpoint of analytical psychology; but so far I have remained only on the surface. We can go very much deeper if we apply the methods of investigation used in analytical psychology. The practical application of these would be out of the question for the ordinary teacher, and an amateurish or half-serious use of them is to be severely discouraged, although some knowledge of them on the part of the teacher is certainly desirable. It is by no means desirable, however, that he should apply them directly to the education of the children. It is his own education that needs them, and this will eventually redound to the good of his pupils.

109   You may perhaps be surprised to hear me speak of the education of the educator, but I must tell you that I am far from thinking that a man's education is completed when he leaves school, even if he has achieved the university grade. There should be not only continuation courses for young people, but continuation schools for adults. At present we educate people only up to the point where they can earn a living and marry; then education ceases altogether, as though a complete mental outfit had been acquired. The solution of all the remaining complicated problems of life is left to the discretion—and ignorance—of the individual. Innumerable ill-advised and unhappy marriages, innumerable professional disappointments, are due solely to this lack of adult education. Vast numbers of men and women thus spend their entire lives in complete ignorance of the most important things. Many childish vices are believed to be ineradicable, largely because they are often found in adults whose education is supposed to be finished, and who are therefore thought to be long past the educable period. There was never a greater mistake. The adult *is* educable, and can respond gratefully to the art of individual education; but naturally his education cannot be conducted along the lines suitable to the child. He has lost the extraordinary plasticity of the child's mind, and has acquired a will of his own, personal convictions, and a more or less definite consciousness of himself, so that he is far less amenable to systematic influence. To this must be

57

added the fact that the child, in his psychic development, passes through the ancestral stages and is only educated up to the modern level of culture and consciousness. The adult, however, stands firmly on this level and feels himself to be the upholder of contemporary culture. He therefore has little inclination to submit to a teacher like a child. As a matter of fact, it is important that he should not submit, otherwise he might easily slip back into a childish state of dependence.

110   The educational method, then, that will best meet the needs of the adult must be indirect rather than direct; that is to say, it must put him in possession of such psychological knowledge as will permit him to educate himself. Such an effort could not and should not be expected from a child, but we can expect it from an adult, especially if he is a teacher. The teacher must not be a merely passive upholder of culture; he must actively promote that culture through his own self-education. His culture must never remain at a standstill, otherwise he will start correcting in the children those faults which he has neglected in himself. This is manifestly the antithesis of education.

111   Analytical psychology has given considerable thought to the methods for aiding the adult in his psychic growth, but if I speak to you about them now, it is for the sole purpose of making clear the possibilities of continued self-education. I must warn you again most emphatically that it would be very unsound to apply these methods directly to children. The indispensable basis of self-education is self-knowledge. We gain self-knowledge partly from a critical survey and judgment of our own actions, and partly from the criticism of others. Self-criticism, however, is all too prone to personal prejudice, while criticism from others is liable to err or to be otherwise displeasing to us. At all events, the self-knowledge accruing to us from these two sources is incomplete and confused like all human judgments, which are seldom free from the falsifications of desire and fear. But is there not some objective critique which will tell us what we really are, somewhat after the fashion, say, of a thermometer, which confronts the fever patient with the indisputable fact that he has a temperature of exactly 103.1°? Where our bodies are concerned we do not deny the existence of objective criteria. If, for example, we are convinced that we can eat strawberries, like everybody else, without ill effects, and the body nevertheless reacts

with a violent rash, this is objective proof that despite our idea to the contrary we are allergic to strawberries.

112   But when it comes to psychology, it seems to us that everything is voluntary and subject to our choice. This universal prejudice arises from our tendency to identify the whole psyche with the conscious phase of it. There are, however, many extremely important psychic processes which are unconscious, or only indirectly conscious. Of the unconscious we can know nothing directly, but indirectly we can perceive the effects that come into consciousness. If everything in consciousness were, as it seems, subject to our will and choice, then we could not discover anywhere an objective criterion by which to test our self-knowledge. Yet there is something independent of desire and fear, something as impersonal as a product of nature, that enables us to know the truth about ourselves. This objective statement is to be found in a product of psychic activity which is the very last thing we would credit with such a meaning, namely the dream.

113   What are dreams? Dreams are products of unconscious psychic activity occurring during sleep. In this condition the mind is to a large extent withdrawn from our voluntary control. With the small portion of consciousness that remains to us in the dream state we apperceive what is going on, but we are no longer in a position to guide the course of psychic events according to our wish and purpose; hence we are also robbed of the possibility of deceiving ourselves. The dream is a spontaneous process resulting from the independent activity of the unconscious, and is as far removed from our conscious control as, shall we say, the physiological activity of digestion. Therefore, we have in it an absolutely objective process from the nature of which we can draw objective conclusions about the situation as it really is.

114   That is all very well, you will say, but how in the world is it possible to draw trustworthy conclusions from the fortuitous and chaotic confusion of a dream? To this I hasten to reply that dreams are only apparently fortuitous and chaotic. On closer inspection we discover a remarkable sequence in the dream-images, both in relation to one another and in relation to the content of waking consciousness. This discovery was made by means of a relatively simple procedure, which works as follows: The body of the dream is divided into its separate portions or

59

images, and all the free associations to each portion are collected. In doing this, we soon become aware of an extremely intimate connection between the dream-images and the things that occupy our thoughts in the waking state, although the meaning of this connection may not be immediately apparent. By collecting all the associations we complete the preliminary part of the dream analysis, thus establishing the context, which shows the manifold connections of the dream with the contents of consciousness and the intimate way in which it is bound up with the tendencies of the personality.

115   When we have illuminated the dream from all sides we can begin the second part of our task, namely the interpretation of the material before us. Here as everywhere in science, we must rid ourselves of prejudice as far as possible, and let the material speak for itself. In very many cases a single glance at the dream and the assembled material suffices to give us at least an intuition of its meaning, and no special effort of thought is needed to interpret it. In other cases it requires much labour and considerable experience. Unfortunately I cannot enter here into the far-reaching question of dream-symbolism. Massive tomes have been written on this subject, and although in practice we cannot do without the experience stored up in these volumes, there are many cases where sound common sense is enough.

116   By way of illustration I shall now give you a short dream, together with its meaning.

117   The dreamer was a man with an academic education, about fifty years of age. I knew him only slightly, and our occasional meetings consisted mostly of humorous gibes on his part at what we called the "game" of dream interpretation. On one of these occasions he asked me laughingly if I was still at it. I replied that he obviously had a very mistaken idea of the nature of dreams. He then remarked that he had just had a dream which I must interpret for him. I said I would do so, and he told me the following dream:

He was alone in the mountains, and wanted to climb a very high, steep mountain which he could see towering in front of him. At first the ascent was laborious, but then it seemed to him that the higher he climbed the more he felt himself being drawn towards the summit. Faster and faster he climbed, and gradually a sort of ecstasy came over him. He felt he was actually soaring up on wings, and when he reached the top he seemed to weigh nothing at all, and stepped lightly off into empty space. Here he awoke.

118   He wanted to know what I thought of his dream. I knew that he was not only an experienced but an ardent mountain-climber, so I was not surprised to see yet another vindication of the rule that dreams speak the same language as the dreamer. Knowing that mountaineering was such a passion with him, I got him to talk about it. He seized on this eagerly and told me how he loved to go alone without a guide, because the very danger of it had a tremendous fascination for him. He also told me about several dangerous tours, and the daring he displayed made a particular impression on me. I asked myself what it could be that impelled him to seek out such dangerous situations, apparently with an almost morbid enjoyment. Evidently a similar thought occurred to him, for he added, becoming at the same time more serious, that he had no fear of danger, since he thought that death in the mountains would be something very beautiful. This remark threw a significant light on the dream. Obviously he was looking for danger, possibly with the unavowed idea of suicide. But why should he deliberately seek death? There must be some special reason. I therefore threw in the remark that a man in his position ought not to expose himself to such risks. To which he replied very emphatically that he would never "give up his mountains," that he had to go to them in order to get away from the city and his family. "This sticking at home does not suit me," he said. Here was a clue to the deeper reason for his passion. I gathered that his marriage was a failure, and that there was nothing to keep him at home. Also he seemed disgusted with his professional work. It occurred to me that his uncanny passion for the mountains must be an avenue of escape from an existence that had become intolerable to him.

119   I therefore privately interpreted the dream as follows: Since he still clung on to life in spite of himself, the ascent of the mountain was at first laborious. But the more he surrendered himself to his passion, the more it lured him on and lent wings to his feet. Finally it lured him completely out of himself: he lost all sense of bodily weight and climbed even higher than the mountain, out into empty space. Obviously this meant death in the mountains.

120   After a pause, he said suddenly, "Well, we've talked about all sorts of other things. You were going to interpret my dream. What do you think about it?" I told him quite frankly what I thought, namely that he was seeking his death in the mountains, and that with such an attitude he stood a remarkably good chance of finding it.

121   "But that is absurd," he replied, laughing. "On the contrary, I am seeking my health in the mountains."

122   Vainly I tried to make him see the gravity of the situation. Six months later, on the descent from a very dangerous peak, he literally stepped off into space. He fell on the head of a companion who was standing on a ledge below him, and both were killed.[5]

123   From this dream we can observe the general function of dreams. It reflects certain vital tendencies of the personality, either those whose meaning embraces our whole life, or those which are momentarily of most importance. The dream presents an objective statement of these tendencies, a statement unconcerned with our conscious wishes and beliefs. After this you will probably agree with me that a dream may in certain circumstances be of inestimable value for conscious life, even when it is not, as here, a matter of life and death.

124   How much of moral and practical value this dreamer would have gained if only he had known of his dangerous lack of restraint!

125   That is why, as physicians of the soul, we have to turn to the ancient art of dream interpretation. We have to educate adults who are no longer willing, like children, to be guided by authority. We have to do with men and women whose way of life is so individual that no counsellor, however wise, could prescribe the way that is uniquely right for them. Therefore we have to teach them to listen to their own natures, so that they can understand from within themselves what is happening.

126   So far as is possible within the limits of a lecture, I have tried to give you some insight into the world of analytical psychology and its ideas. I for my part shall be satisfied if what I have said is of help to you in your profession.

5 [This case is also discussed in "The Practical Use of Dream Analysis," *Coll. Works,* Vol. 16, pars. 323f., where further details will be found.—EDITORS.]

IV

ANALYTICAL PSYCHOLOGY AND EDUCATION

[The following three lectures were delivered at the International Congress of Education, in London in 1924. They were originally drafted in English by the author and revised by Roberts Aldrich. They were then published in German as *Analytische Psychologie und Erziehung* (Heidelberg, 1926), and the English version was subsequently published in *Contributions to Analytical Psychology* (London and New York, 1928) together with the preceding lecture. The present new translation is made from the revised and enlarged edition of *Psychologie und Erziehung* (Zurich, 1946), on the basis of careful comparison between it and the earlier English version.—EDITORS.]

127   Psychology is one of the youngest sciences. The word "psychology" has been in use for a long time, but formerly it was
only the title of a certain chapter in philosophy—that chapter in
which the philosopher more or less laid down the law as to what
the human soul had to be according to the premises of his own
particular philosophy. I remember, as a young student, that I
used to enjoy the privilege of hearing from one professor how
little was known about the real nature of psychic processes, and
from another exactly what the psyche had to be as a logical
necessity. If one studies the origins of modern empirical psychology one is profoundly impressed by the fight which the earliest
investigators had to wage against the firmly entrenched scholastic
way of thinking. Philosophic thought, powerfully influenced by
theology ("queen of sciences"), had a decidedly deductive tendency, and over it there reigned a mass of naïve, idealistic precon-
ceptions which were bound sooner or later to lead to a reaction.
This reaction took the form of the materialism of the nineteenth
century, from whose outlook we are not yet completely freed
even today. The success of the empirical method is so undeniable
that the splendour of its victory has even begotten a materialistic
philosophy, which in reality is more a psychological reaction
than a justifiable scientific theory. The materialistic outlook is
an exaggerated reaction against the medieval idealism and has
nothing to do with the empirical method as such.

128   Thus modern empirical psychology was cradled in an atmosphere of rank materialism. It was first and foremost a physiological psychology, thoroughly empirical in its experimental
basis, viewing the psychic process exclusively from outside and
mainly with an eye to its physiological manifestations. Such a
state of affairs was fairly satisfactory so long as psychology was
a department of philosophy or of the natural sciences. So long as
it was restricted to the laboratory, psychology could remain
purely experimental and could regard the psychic process entirely from outside. Instead of the old dogmatic psychology we
now had a philosophical psychology no less academic in its origins. However, the peace of the academic laboratory was soon to
be disturbed by the demands of those who needed psychology
for practical purposes. These intruders were the doctors. The
neurologist as well as the psychiatrist has to concern himself
with psychic disorders and therefore feels the urgent need of a
psychology that can be practically applied. Quite independently
of the developments of academic psychology medical men had already discovered a means of access to the human mind and to the
psychological treatment of its disorders. This was hypnotism,
which grew out of what had been called "mesmerism" in the
latter part of the eighteenth century, and "animal magnetism"
at the beginning of the nineteenth. The development of hypnotism led, via Charcot, Liébeault, and Bernheim, to the kind
of medical psychology represented by Pierre Janet. Another of
Charcot's pupils, Freud, in Vienna,[1] used the hypnotic method
at first very much in the same way as Janet, but he soon struck
out on a different path. Whereas Janet remained for the most
part descriptive, Freud penetrated further and more deeply into
matters which, to the medical science of those days, hardly
seemed worth investigating, namely the morbid fantasies of the
patient and their activity in the realm of the unconscious mind.
It would be unjust to imply that Janet overlooked this; indeed
the contrary is the case. It is his great merit to have pointed
out the existence and the importance of unconscious processes
in the psychological structure of nervous and mental disorders.
Freud's particular merit lies not in the actual discovery of unconscious activity, but in unveiling the real nature of this ac-

[1] Freud also translated Hippolyte Bernheim's work into German, under the title
Die Suggestion und ihre Heilwirkung (Leipzig and Vienna, 1888).

tivity, and above all in working out a practical method for exploring the unconscious. Independently of Freud, I too had approached the problem of a practical psychology firstly from the side of experimental psychopathology, employing chiefly the association method, and then from the study of the personality.[2] As Freud made the hitherto neglected morbid fantasies of the patient his special field of research,[3] so I directed my attention more particularly to the reasons why people made certain mistakes in the course of the association experiment. Like the fantasies of hysterics, the disturbances in the association experiment were regarded as valueless and meaningless, a purely fortuitous phenomenon, in a word, as so much *materia vilis*. I discovered,[4] however, that these disturbances were due to the operation of unconscious processes which I called "feeling-toned complexes."[5] After having, so to speak, put my finger on the same psychological mechanisms as Freud, it was natural that I should become his pupil and collaborator over a period of many years. But while I always recognized the truth of his conclusions so far as the facts were concerned, I could not conceal my doubts as to the validity of his theories. His regrettable dogmatism was the main reason why I felt obliged to part company from him. My scientific conscience would not allow me to lend support to an almost fanatical dogma based on a one-sided interpretation of the facts.

129   Freud's achievement is by no means inconsiderable. But while he shares with others the discovery of the unconscious in relation to the aetiology and structure of neuroses and psychoses, his great and unique merit, to my mind, lies in his discovery of a method for exploring the unconscious and, more particularly, dreams. He was the first to make the bold attempt to

2 Cf. my dissertation, "On the Psychology and Pathology of So-called Occult Phenomena," *Coll. Works,* Vol 1.

3 See his *Collected Papers* (London, 1924–50), Vols. II and III.

4 The results of my own experiments and those of my fellow workers are set forth in *Studies in Word Association,* trans. by M. D. Eder (London, 1918; New York, 1919). [Professor Jung's contributions to this volume appear in *Coll. Works,* Vol. 2. —EDITORS.]

5 The so-called "complex theory" found its application in the psychopathology of schizophrenia (cf. my *The Psychology of Dementia Praecox, Coll. Works,* Vol. 3). An account of the same appears in "A Review of the Complex Theory," *Coll. Works,* Vol. 8.

throw open the secret doors of the dream. The discovery that dreams have a meaning, and that there is a way to an understanding of them, is perhaps the most significant and most valuable part of this remarkable edifice called psychoanalysis. I do not wish to belittle Freud's achievement, but I feel I must be fair to all those who have wrestled with the great problems of medical psychology and who, through their labours, have laid the foundations without which neither Freud nor myself would have been able to accomplish our tasks. Thus Pierre Janet, Auguste Forel, Théodore Flournoy, Morton Prince, Eugen Bleuler, deserve gratitude and remembrance whenever we speak of the first steps of medical psychology.

130   Freud's work has shown that the functional neuroses are causally based on unconscious contents whose nature, when understood, allows us to see how the disease came about. The value of this discovery is as great as the discovery of the specific cause of tuberculosis and other infectious diseases. Moreover, quite apart from the therapeutic importance of analytical psychology, the psychology of the normal has been tremendously enriched, for the understanding of dreams has opened up an almost limitless vista, showing how consciousness develops out of the remotest and darkest depths of the unconscious, while the practical application of the analytical method has enabled us to distinguish typical functions and attitudes in the behaviour of normal individuals. In so far as psychoanalysis is a branch of medical psychology, it concerns itself solely with abnormal cases and should therefore be reserved for the physician; but dream psychology, studied for the light it throws upon normal human behaviour, will be of ever-increasing interest to thoughtful people generally, and especially to those with educational inclinations. It is in fact highly desirable that the educator, if he wishes really to understand the mentality of his pupils, should pay attention to the findings of analytical psychology. That, however, presupposes some knowledge of psychopathology, for the abnormal child is far harder to understand than the normal. Abnormality and disease are not far apart, and just as one expects some knowledge of the physical ailments of children from the all-round educated teacher, so one might expect from him a little knowledge of their psychic ailments.

131   There are five main groups of psychic disturbances in children:

BACKWARD CHILDREN. A common form of backward child is the mental defective, characterized chiefly by low intelligence and a general incapacity to understand.

132   The most obvious type is the phlegmatic, slow, dull-witted, stupid child. Among these cases may be found children who, for all their poverty of intellect, are distinguished by a certain richness of heart, and who are capable of loyalty, affection, devotion, reliability, and self-sacrifice. The less obvious and rarer type is the excitable, easily irritated child, whose mental incapacity is no less indubitable than that of the defective, but is often markedly one-sided.

133   From these congenital and practically incurable, though not ineducable, types we must distinguish the child with arrested mental development. His development is very slow, at times almost imperceptible, and it often needs the expert diagnosis of a skilled psychiatrist to decide whether it is a case of mental defect or not. Such children frequently have the emotional reactions of imbeciles. I was once consulted about a boy of six years old who suffered from violent fits of rage, during which he used to smash his toys and threaten his parents and his nurse in quite a dangerous way. In addition he "refused to speak," as his parents put it. He was a little fellow, well-fed, but terribly suspicious, malevolent, obstinate, and altogether negative. It was perfectly obvious that he was an imbecile and simply *could* not speak. He had never learnt how to do so. But his imbecility was not bad enough to account entirely for his inability to speak. His general behaviour pointed to a neurosis. Whenever a young child exhibits the symptoms of a neurosis one should not waste too much time examining his unconscious. One should begin one's investigations elsewhere, starting with the mother; for almost invariably the parents are either the direct cause of the child's neurosis or at least the most important element in it. Thus I found that the child was the only boy among seven girls. The mother was an ambitious, self-willed woman, who took it as an insult when I told her that her son was not normal. She had deliberately repressed all knowledge of the boy's infirmity; he simply *had* to be intelligent, and if he was stupid, it was all due to his evil will and malicious obstinacy. Naturally the boy learnt far less than

he would have done had he been lucky enough to possess a reasonable mother; in fact he learnt nothing at all. What is more, he duly became the very things his mother's own ambition drove him to, namely, malicious and self-willed. Totally misunderstood, and therefore isolated within himself, he developed his fits of rage out of sheer despair. I know of another boy, of fourteen, in much the same family circumstances. He killed his stepfather with an axe during a paroxysm of rage. He too had been pushed too far.

134 Arrested mental development is found not infrequently in first children, or in children whose parents are estranged through psychic incompatibilities. It may also result from the mother's illness during pregnancy, or from prolonged labour, or from deformation of the skull and hemorrhage during delivery. If such children are not ruined by educational forcing, they normally attain a relative mental maturity in the course of time, though it may be later than with ordinary children.

135 The second group comprises PSYCHOPATHIC CHILDREN. In cases of moral insanity the disorder is either congenital or due to organic injury of parts of the brain by wounding or disease. Such cases are incurable. Occasionally they become criminals and they have in them the seeds of habitual criminality.

136 From this group one must carefully distinguish the child with arrested moral development, the morbidly autoerotic type. These cases often display an alarming amount of egotism and premature sexual activity; in addition they are untruthful and unreliable, and almost completely lacking in human feeling and love. As a rule they are illegitimate or adopted children who have unfortunately never been warmed and nourished by the psychic atmosphere of a real father and mother. They suffer from an almost organic lack of something that every child needs as a vital necessity, namely the psychically nourishing care of parents, and especially of a mother. As a result, illegitimate children in particular are always exposed to psychic danger, and it is the moral sphere that suffers first and foremost. Many children can adapt to foster parents, but not all; and those who cannot, develop an extremely self-centred and ruthlessly egotistical attitude for the unconscious purpose of getting for themselves what the real parents have failed to give them. Such cases are not always incurable. I once saw a boy who violated his four-year-old

sister when he was five, tried to kill his father when he was nine, but at the age of eighteen was developing into satisfactory normality, despite a diagnosis of incurable moral insanity. If the unbridled licentiousness to which such cases are sometimes prone is coupled with a good intelligence, and if there is no irreparable break with society, these patients can give up their criminal tendencies by using their heads. Nevertheless, it is to be observed that reason is a very flimsy barrier against pathological proclivities.

137   The third group consists of EPILEPTIC CHILDREN. These cases are unfortunately not uncommon. It is easy enough to recognize a true epileptic attack, but what is called "petit mal" is an exceedingly obscure and complicated condition. Here there are no obvious attacks, only very peculiar and often hardly perceptible alterations of consciousness, which nevertheless pass over into the severe mental disorder of the epileptic with his irritability, ferocity, greediness, his sticky sentimentality, his morbid passion for justice, his egotism, and his narrow range of interests. It is of course impossible to enumerate here all the manifold forms of epilepsy; but, in order to illustrate its symptomatology, I will mention the case of a small boy who began to behave strangely when he was about seven years old. The first thing to be noticed was that he used to disappear abruptly, and was then found hiding in the cellar or in a dark corner of the attic. It was impossible to get him to explain why he ran away so suddenly and hid himself. Sometimes he would leave off playing and bury his face in his mother's skirts. At first these things happened so rarely that no attention was paid to his odd behaviour, but when he began to do the same thing at school, suddenly leaving his desk and running to the teacher, his family became alarmed. Nobody, however, had thought of the possibility of a serious disease. Occasionally, too, he would stop short for a few seconds in the middle of a game, or even in the middle of a sentence, without any explanation and apparently without even knowing that the lapse had occurred. Gradually he developed a rather disagreeable and irritable character. Sometimes he had fits of rage, and on one occasion he threw a pair of scissors at his little sister with such force that the point pierced the bone of the skull just above the eyes, nearly killing her. As the parents did not think of consulting a psychiatrist, the disease remained un-

recognized, and he was treated simply as a bad boy. At the age of twelve he had his first observed epileptic fit, and only then was his disease understood. Despite great difficulties I was able to find out from the boy that when he was about six he began to be seized with terror of some unknown being. When he was alone, he had the feeling that someone unseen was present. Later he came to see a short man with a beard, a man he had never seen before, but whose features he could describe in great detail. This man suddenly appeared before him and frightened him so much that he ran away and hid himself. It was difficult to discover why the man was so terrifying. The boy was obviously upset about something, which he treated as a dreadful secret. It took me hours to win his confidence, but eventually he confessed. "This man tried to make me take something terrible from him. I can't tell you what it was, it was frightful. He came nearer and nearer and kept on insisting that I must take it, but I was so frightened that I always ran away and did not take it." As he said this he turned pale and began to tremble with fear. When at last I succeeded in calming him down, he said, "This man tried to make me take a *sin*." "But what sort of a sin?" I asked. The boy stood up, looked suspiciously all round him, and then whispered, "It was murder." When he was eight years old he had, as I mentioned above, made a violent attack on his sister. Later, the attacks of fear continued, but the vision changed. The terrible man did not return; but in his stead there appeared the figure of a nun, a sort of nurse. At first her face was veiled, but later it was unveiled, revealing a most terrifying expression, a pale, deathlike face. Between the ages of nine and twelve he was haunted by this figure. The fits of rage, despite his growing irritability, ceased, but the manifest epileptic attacks began to appear instead. Clearly, the vision of the nun signified the changing of the incompatible criminal tendency symbolized by the bearded man into obvious disease.[6]

138   Sometimes such cases are still mainly functional and not yet organic, so that it is possible to do something for them with psychotherapy. That is why I have mentioned this case in some

[6] It is interesting to see how the subliminally existing murder which was seeking to attach itself to the patient in later life (bearded man) is compensated by the disease (the nurse), as if the disease were protecting him against the crime.

detail. It may give some idea of what goes on in the child's mind behind the scenes.

139   The fourth group comprises the various forms of PSYCHOSIS. Although such cases are not common among children, one can find at least the first stages of that pathological mental development which later, after puberty, leads to schizophrenia in all its manifold forms. As a rule these children behave in a strange and even bizarre way; they are incomprehensible, often quite un-get-at-able, hypersensitive, shut in, emotionally abnormal, being either torpid or liable to explode over the most trifling causes.

140   I once had to examine a boy of fourteen in whom sexual activity had begun suddenly and somewhat prematurely in a rather disquieting way, so that it disturbed his sleep and upset his general health. The trouble began when the boy went to a dance and a certain girl refused to dance with him. He went away in high dudgeon. When he got home he tried to learn his school lessons, but found it was impossible because of a mounting and indescribable emotion compounded of fear, rage, and despair, which took hold of him more and more until at last he rushed out into the garden and rolled on the ground in an almost unconscious condition. After a couple of hours the emotion passed and the sexual trouble began. There were several cases of schizophrenia in this boy's family. This is a typical pathological emotion characteristic of children with a bad family inheritance.

141   The fifth group consists of NEUROTIC CHILDREN. It is of course quite beyond the scope of a single lecture to describe all the symptoms and forms of a childhood neurosis. Anything may be found, ranging from abnormally naughty behaviour to definitely hysterical attacks and states. The trouble can be apparently physical, for instance hysterical fever or abnormally low temperature, convulsions, paralysis, pain, digestive disturbances, etc., or it can be mental and moral, taking the form of excitement or depression, lying, sexual perversion, stealing, and so forth. I remember the case of a little girl of four who had suffered from the most chronic constipation since the first year of her life. She had already undergone every imaginable and unimaginable kind of physical treatment. All were useless, because the doctors overlooked the one important factor in the

73

child's life, namely her mother. As soon as I saw the mother I realized that she was the real cause, and so I suggested treating her and advised her at the same time to give up the child. Another person took the mother's place, and the next day the trouble was gone, and did not return, as I was able to follow up the case for many years afterward. The solution of this problem was quite simple as regards the child, though of course it would not have been so had not the pathogenic influence coming from the mother been removed through analysis. The little girl was a youngest child, the regular pet of a neurotic mother. The latter projected all her phobias onto the child and surrounded her with so much anxious care that she was never free from tension, and such a state is notoriously unfavourable to the peristaltic function.

142   It is my conviction that it is absolutely essential for any teacher who wishes to apply the principles of analytical psychology to have a first-hand knowledge of the psychopathology of childhood and its attendant dangers. Unfortunately, there are certain books on psychoanalysis which give the impression that it is all very simple and that success can be had for the asking. No competent psychiatrist could endorse such superficial notions, and no warning can be too emphatic against unskilled and frivolous attempts to analyse children. There is no doubt that it is of the greatest value to the educator to know what modern psychology has contributed to the understanding of the child mind. But anyone who wishes to apply analytical methods to children must have thorough knowledge of the pathological conditions he will be called upon to deal with. I must confess that I do not see how anyone, except a responsible physician, can dare to analyse children without special knowledge and medical advice.

143   To analyse children is a most difficult and delicate task. The conditions under which we have to work are altogether different from those governing the analysis of grown-ups. The child has a special psychology. Just as its body during the embryonic period is part of the mother's body, so its mind is for many years part of the parents' mental atmosphere. That explains why so many neuroses of children are more symptoms of the mental condition of the parents than a genuine illness of the child. Only a very little of the child's psychic life is its own; for the most

part it is still dependent on that of the parents. Such dependence is normal, and to disturb it is injurious to the natural growth of the child's mind. It is therefore understandable that premature and indelicate enlightenment on the facts of sex can have a disastrous effect on his relations with his parents, and such an effect is almost inevitable if you base your analysis on the dogma that the relations between parents and children are necessarily sexual.

144　　It is no less unjustifiable to give the so-called Oedipus complex the status of a prime cause. The Oedipus complex is a symptom. Just as any strong attachment to a person or a thing may be described as a "marriage," and just as the primitive mind can express almost anything by using a sexual metaphor, so the regressive tendency of a child may be described in sexual terms as an "incestuous longing for the mother." But it is no more than a figurative way of speaking. The word "incest" has a definite meaning, and designates a definite thing, and as a general rule can only be applied to an adult who is psychologically incapable of linking his sexuality to its proper object. To apply the same term to the difficulties in the development of a child's consciousness is highly misleading.

145　　This is not to say that sexual precocity does not exist. But such cases are distinctly exceptional and abnormal, and there is nothing to justify the doctor in extending the concepts of pathology to the sphere of the normal. Just as it is hardly permissible to call blushing a skin disease, or joy a fit of madness, so cruelty is not necessarily sadism, pleasure is not necessarily lust, and firmness is not necessarily sexual repression.

146　　In studying the history of the human mind one is impressed again and again by the fact that its growth keeps pace with a widening range of consciousness, and that each step forward is an extremely painful and laborious achievement. One could almost say that nothing is more hateful to man than to give up the smallest particle of unconsciousness. He has a profound fear of the unknown. Ask anybody who has ever tried to introduce new ideas! If even the allegedly mature man is afraid of the unknown, why shouldn't the child hesitate also? The *horror novi* is one of the most striking qualities of primitive man. This is a natural enough obstacle, as obstacles go; but excessive attachment to the parents is unnatural and pathological, because a too

75

great fear of the unknown is itself pathological. Hence one should avoid the one-sided conclusion that hesitation in advancing is necessarily due to sexual dependence on the parents. Often it may be simply a *reculer pour mieux sauter*. Even in cases where children do exhibit sexual symptoms—where, in other words, the incestuous tendency is perfectly obvious—I should recommend a careful examination of the parents' psyche. One finds astonishing things, such as a father unconsciously in love with his own daughter, a mother who is unconsciously flirting with her son, imputing under the cover of unconsciousness their own adult emotions to their children, who, again unconsciously, act the parts allotted to them. Children will not of course play these strange and unnatural roles unless unconsciously forced into them by their parents' attitude.

147   I will now describe one such case. There was a family of four children, two daughters and two sons. All four were neurotic. The girls had shown neurotic symptoms since before puberty. I shall avoid unnecessary details, sketching the fate of the family only in broad outline.

148   The elder daughter, when she was twenty, fell in love with an eminently suitable young man of good family and a university education. The marriage, however, was put off for one reason or another, and, as though hypnotized, she started an affair with one of her father's office employees. She seemed to love her fiancé very much, but was so prudish with him that she never allowed him even to kiss her, while she went very far with the other man without the slightest hesitation. She was excessively naïve and childish, and totally unconscious at first of what she was doing. Then, to her unspeakable horror, the full consciousness of it came over her. She broke down completely, and for years she suffered from hysteria. She severed her connection with the employee and also with her fiancé without explaining her conduct to anyone.

149   The second daughter got married, apparently with no difficulties, but to a man below her mental level. She was frigid and remained childless. In less than a year she had fallen so passionately in love with a friend of her husband's that it developed into a long-drawn-out love affair.

150   The elder son, in himself a talented young man, showed the first signs of neurotic indecision when it came to choosing a

career. Eventually he decided to study chemistry, but he had no sooner begun than he was overwhelmed with such a homesickness that he left the university and went straight home to mother. There he fell into a peculiar state of mental confusion with hallucinations, and when this state subsided again after about six weeks, he resolved to take up medicine. He actually went so far as to sit for the examination. Soon afterwards he became engaged. Hardly was the engagement a fact than he began to doubt the rightness of his choice; then came anxiety states and the engagement was broken off. Thereupon he went right off his head and had to be shut up in an asylum for several months.

151   The second son was a psychasthenic neurotic, a woman-hater who seriously planned to remain a bachelor all his life and clung to his mother in the most sentimental way.

152   I was called in to deal with all four children. In each case the history pointed back unmistakably to the mother's secret. Eventually I learned her story. She was a talented, vivacious woman, who in her young days had received a strict, very one-sided and narrow education. With the utmost severity towards herself and with remarkable strength of character she had adhered all her life to the principles implanted in her, and allowed herself no exceptions. She had not long been married when she got to know a friend of her husband's, and fell obviously in love with him. It was equally obvious to her that this love was fully reciprocated. But her principles made no provision for such an eventuality, therefore it had no right to exist. She always behaved as if nothing were amiss, and she kept up the part for over twenty years until the death of this man, with never a word spoken on either side. Her relations with her husband were distant and correct. In later years she suffered from periodic melancholia.

153   Naturally such a state of affairs could not fail to create a very oppressive atmosphere in the home, and nothing influences children more than these silent facts in the background. They have an extremely contagious effect on the children. The daughters unconsciously imitated their mother's attitude,[7] while the sons sought compensation by remaining, as it were, unconscious

[7] Cf. my "The Psychological Aspects of the Mother Archetype," *Coll. Works*, Vol. 9, and "Mind and Earth," *Coll. Works*, Vol. 10.

lovers, the unconscious love being over-compensated by their conscious rejection of women.

154   As one can imagine, it is not at all easy in practice to deal with such cases. Treatment should really have begun with the mother, or rather with the relations between the father and the mother. I think that an all-round conscious realization of the situation and its implications would have had a salutary effect. Conscious realization prevents the unmentionable atmosphere, the general cluelessness, the blank disregard of the troublesome object; in short, it stops the painful content from being repressed. And though this may seem to cause the individual more suffering, he is at least suffering meaningfully and from something real. Repression has the apparent advantage of clearing the conscious mind of worry, and the spirit of all its troubles, but, to counter that, it causes an indirect suffering from something unreal, namely a neurosis. Neurotic suffering is an unconscious fraud and has no moral merit, as has real suffering. Apart, however, from producing a neurosis the repressed cause of the suffering has other effects: it radiates out into the environment and, if there are children, infects them too. In this way neurotic states are often passed on from generation to generation, like the curse of Atreus. The children are infected indirectly through the attitude they instinctively adopt towards their parents' state of mind: either they fight against it with unspoken protest (though occasionally the protest is vociferous) or else they succumb to a paralysing and compulsive imitation. In both cases they are obliged to do, to feel, and to live not as *they* want, but as their parents want. The more "impressive" the parents are, and the less they accept their own problems (mostly on the excuse of "sparing the children"), the longer the children will have to suffer from the unlived life of their parents and the more they will be forced into fulfilling all the things the parents have repressed and kept unconscious. It is not a question of the parents having to be "perfect" in order to have no deleterious effects on their children. If they really were perfect, it would be a positive catastrophe, for the children would then have no alternative but moral inferiority, unless of course they chose to fight the parents with their own weapons, that is, copy them. But this trick only postpones the final reckoning till the third generation. The repressed problems and the suffering thus

fraudulently avoided secrete an insidious poison which seeps into the soul of the child through the thickest walls of silence and through the whited sepulchres of deceit, complacency, and evasion. The child is helplessly exposed to the psychic influence of the parents and is bound to copy their self-deception, their insincerity, hypocrisy, cowardice, self-righteousness, and selfish regard for their own comfort, just as wax takes up the imprint of the seal. The only thing that can save the child from unnatural injury is the efforts of the parents not to shirk the psychic difficulties of life by deceitful manoeuvres or by remaining artificially unconscious, but rather to accept them as tasks, to be as honest with themselves as possible, and to shed a beam of light into the darkest corners of their souls. If they can confess to an understanding ear, so much the better. If for certain reasons they cannot, that is admittedly an aggravation, but not a disadvantage—on the contrary, it is often an advantage, for they are then forced to cope unaided with the thing that is most difficult for them. Public confession, as in the Salvation Army or the Oxford Group, is extremely effective for simple souls who can unbosom themselves *ex profundis*. But such souls are not exactly at home in a fashionable drawing-room, nor are such confessions to be heard there, however indiscreet. Confession, as we know, can also be used for self-deception. The more intelligent and cultured a man is, the more subtly he can humbug himself. No moderately intelligent person should believe himself either a saint or a sinner. Both would be a conscious lie. Rather he should keep shamefacedly silent about his moral qualities, ever mindful of his abysmal sinfulness on the one hand, and of his meritoriously humble insight into this desolate state of affairs on the other. All that the younger Blumhardt [8] remarked to an acquaintance of mine, on his making an agonizingly contrite confession of sin, was: "Do you think God is interested in your miserable muck?" Blumhardt had evidently noted the trick that makes drawing-room confession so attractive.

155   It is not, let me repeat, a question of the parents committing no faults—that would be humanly impossible—but of their recognizing them for what they are. It is not life that must be checked,

8 [Christoph Blumhardt (1842–1919), eminent Swiss theologian and Social Democrat.—EDITORS.]

but unconsciousness; above all, the unconsciousness of the educator. But that means our own unconsciousness, because each one of us is, for better or worse, the educator of his fellow man. For so morally bound up with one another are we human beings that a leader leads the led, and the led mislead the leader.

156   Scientific psychology, to begin with, was either physiological psychology, or a rather unorganized accumulation of observations and experiments dealing with isolated facts and functions. Freud's hypothesis, though certainly one-sided, gave it a liberating push towards a psychology of psychic complexities. His work is really a psychology of the ramifications of the sexual instinct in the human psyche. But despite the undeniable importance of sex, one should not suppose that sex is everything. Such a broad hypothesis is like wearing coloured spectacles: it obliterates the finer shades so that everything is seen under the same lurid hue. It is therefore significant that Freud's first pupil, Alfred Adler, framed an entirely different hypothesis of equally broad applicability. The Freudians usually fail to mention Adler's merits, as they make a fanatical creed of their sex-hypothesis. But fanaticism is always a compensation for hidden doubt. Religious persecutions occur only where heresy is a menace. There is no instinct in man that is not balanced by another instinct. Sex would be absolutely unchecked in man were there not a balancing factor in the form of an equally important instinct destined to counteract an unbridled and therefore destructive functioning of the sexual instinct. The structure of the psyche is not unipolar. Just as sex is a force that sways man with its compelling impulses, so there is a natural force of self-assertion in him which enables him to resist emotional explosions. Even among primitives we find the severest restrictions

imposed not only on sex but on other instincts too, without there being any need of the Ten Commandments or of the precepts of the catechism. All restrictions on the blind operation of sex derive from the instinct of self-preservation, which is what Adler's self-assertion amounts to in practice. Unfortunately, Adler in his turn goes too far and, by almost entirely neglecting the Freudian point of view, falls into the same error of one-sidedness and exaggeration. His psychology is the psychology of all the self-assertive tendencies in the human psyche. I admit that a one-sided truth has the advantage of simplicity, but whether it is an adequate hypothesis is another matter. We ought to be able to see that there is much in the psyche that depends on sex—sometimes, indeed, everything; but that at other times very little depends on sex and nearly everything on the instinct of self-preservation, or the power instinct, as Adler called it. Both Freud and Adler make the mistake of assuming the continuous operation of one and the same instinct, as though it were a chemical component that was always present in the same quantity, like the two hydrogen atoms in water. If that were the case, man would be mainly sexual, according to Freud, and mainly self-assertive, according to Adler. But he cannot be both at the same time. Everyone knows that the instincts vary in intensity. Sometimes sex predominates, sometimes self-assertion or some other instinct. That is the simple fact which both investigators have overlooked. When sex predominates, everything becomes sexualized, since everything then expresses or serves the sexual purpose. When hunger predominates, practically everything has to be explained in terms of food. Why do we say, "Don't take him seriously, it's his bad day today"? Because we know that a man's psychology can be profoundly altered by a bad mood. This is even more true when dealing with powerful instincts. Freud and Adler can easily be reconciled if only we will take the trouble to regard the psyche not as a rigid and unalterable system, but as a fluid stream of events which change kaleidoscopically under the alternating influence of different instincts. Hence we may have to explain a man on the Freudian basis before his marriage, and on the Adlerian basis afterwards, which common sense has done all along.[1] Such

[1] Or, to quote the words of a philosopher: "Before supper I am a Kantian, after supper a Nietzschean."

a combination, however, leaves us in a rather uncomfortable situation. Instead of enjoying the apparent certainty of a single, simple truth, we feel ourselves castaways on a boundless sea of ever-changing conditions, helplessly tossed from one vagary to the next. The protean life of the psyche is a greater, if more inconvenient, truth than the rigid certainty of the one-eyed point of view. It certainly does not make the problems of psychology any easier. But it does free us from the incubus of "nothing but," which is the insistent leitmotiv of all one-sidedness.

157　　As soon as the discussion comes to grips with the problem of instinct, everything gets into a dreadful muddle. How are we to distinguish the instincts from one another? How many instincts are there? What are instincts anyway? Thus you immediately get involved in biology and find yourself in more of a muddle than ever. I would therefore advise restriction to the psychological sphere without any assumptions as to the nature of the underlying biological process. The day may come when the biologist, and maybe even the physiologist, will be able to reach out his hand to the psychologist at the point where they meet after tunnelling from opposite sides through the mountain of the unknown.[2] In the meantime, we must learn to be a little more modest in the face of the psychological facts: instead of knowing so exactly that certain things are "nothing but" sex or "nothing but" the will to power, we should take them more at their face value. Consider religious experience, for instance. Can science be so sure that there is no such thing as a "religious instinct"? Can we really suppose that the religious phenomenon is nothing but a secondary function based on the repression of sex? Can anyone show us those "normal" peoples or races who are free from such silly repressions? But if no one can point to any race, or even a tribe, which is quite free from religious phenomena, then I really do not see how one can justify the argument that religious phenomena are not genuine and are merely repressions of sex? Moreover, has not history provided us with plenty of examples where sex is actually an integral part of religious experience? The same is true of art, which is likewise supposed to be the result of sexual repressions, although even animals have aesthetic and artistic instincts. This ridicu-

[2] A very promising beginning has been made in the excellent work of Walter H. von Wyss: *Psychophysiologische Probleme in der Medizin* (Basel, 1944).

lous and well-nigh pathological exaggeration of the importance of sex is itself a symptom of the contemporary spiritual unbalance, owing chiefly to the fact that our age lacks a true understanding of sexuality.[3] Whenever an instinct has been underrated, an abnormal overvaluation is bound to follow. And the more unjust the undervaluation the more unhealthy the subsequent overvaluation. As a matter of fact, no moral condemnation could make sex as hateful as the obscenity and blatant vulgarity of those who exaggerate its importance. The intellectual crudeness of the sexual interpretation makes a right valuation of sex impossible. Thus, probably very much against the personal aspirations of Freud himself, the literature that has followed in his wake is effectively carrying on the work of repression. Before Freud nothing was allowed to be sexual, now everything is nothing but sexual.

158   The preoccupation with sex in psychotherapy is due firstly to the assumption that fixation to the parental imagos is by nature sexual, and secondly to the fact that with many patients sexual fantasies, or those that appear to be such, predominate. Freudian doctrine explains all this in the well-known sexual manner with the laudable intent of freeing the patient from his so-called "sexual" fixation to the parental imagos and initiating him into "normal" life. It speaks, plainly enough, the same language as the patient,[4] and in suitable cases this is of course a distinct advantage, though it becomes a disadvantage as time goes on, because the sexual terminology and ideology bind the problem down to the very level on which it has shown itself to be insoluble. The parents are not just "sexual objects" or "pleasure objects" to be dismissed out of hand; they are, or they represent, vital forces which accompany the child on the winding path of destiny in the form of favourable or dangerous factors, from whose influence even the adult can escape only in limited degree, analysis or no analysis. Father and mother are, whether we know it or not, replaced by something analogous to them— if, that is to say, we succeed in detaching ourselves from them at all. The detachment is possible only if we can step on to the next level. For example, the place of the father is now taken by the

---

[3] [Professor Jung elaborates this theme in "Sigmund Freud: A Cultural Phenomenon," Coll. Works, Vol. 15.—EDITORS.]

[4] Where this fails to work it is put down to the patient's "resistances."

doctor, a phenomenon which Freud called the "transference." But in the place of the mother there is substituted the wisdom of a doctrine. And indeed the great prototype in the Middle Ages was the substitution of Mother Church for the family. In recent times worldly allegiances have taken the place of the spiritual organization of society, for to remain a permanent member of the family has very undesirable psychic consequences and is for that reason rendered impossible even in primitive society by the initiation ceremonies. Man needs a wider community than the family, in whose leading-strings he will be stunted both spiritually and morally. If he is burdened with too much family, if, in later life, his tie to the parents is too strong, he will simply transfer the parental tie to the family he himself has raised (if he ever gets that far), thus creating for his own progeny the same suffocating psychic atmosphere from which he suffered in his youth.

159   No psychic allegiance to any kind of secular organization can ever satisfy the spiritual and emotional demands previously made on the parents. Moreover, it is by no means to the advantage of a secular organization to possess members who make such demands. One can see this clearly enough from the thoughtless expectations which the spiritually immature cherish in regard to "Father State"; and where such misguided yearnings ultimately lead is shown by those countries whose leaders, skilfully exploiting the infantile hopes of the masses by suggestion, have actually succeeded in arrogating to themselves the power and authority of the father. Spiritual impoverishment, stultification, and moral degeneracy have taken the place of spiritual and moral fitness, and produced a mass psychosis that can only lead to disaster. A man cannot properly fulfil even the biological meaning of human existence if this and this only is held up to him as an ideal. Whatever the shortsighted and doctrinaire rationalist may say about the meaning of culture, the fact remains that there is a culture-creating spirit. This spirit is a living spirit and not a mere rationalizing intellect. Accordingly, it makes use of a religious symbolism superordinate to reason, and where this symbolism is lacking or has met with incomprehension, things can only go badly with us. Once we have lost the capacity to orient ourselves by religious truth, there is absolutely nothing which can deliver man from his original

biological bondage to the family, as he will simply transfer his infantile principles, uncorrected, to the world at large, and will find there a father who, so far from guiding him, leads him to perdition. Important as it is for a man to be able to earn his daily bread and if possible to support a family, he will have achieved nothing that could give his life its full meaning. He will not even be able to bring his children up properly, and will thus have neglected to take care of the brood, which is an un-doubted biological ideal. A spiritual goal that points beyond the purely natural man and his worldly existence is an absolute necessity for the health of the soul; it is the Archimedean point from which alone it is possible to lift the world off its hinges and to transform the natural state into a cultural one.

60   Our psychology takes account of the cultural as well as the natural man, and accordingly its explanations must keep both points of view in mind, the spiritual and the biological. As a medical psychology, it cannot do otherwise than pay attention to the whole man. Since the average doctor has been educated exclusively in the natural sciences and is, therefore, accustomed to see everything as a "natural" phenomenon, it is only to be expected that he will understand psychic phenomena from the same biological angle. This mode of observation has great heuristic value and opens out perspectives which were closed to all ages before us. Thanks to its empirical and phenomenolog-ical outlook we now know the facts as they really are; we know what is happening and how it happens, unlike earlier ages which usually had only doctrines and theories about the un-known. One can hardly overestimate the value of strictly scien-tific biological inquiry; it more than anything else has sharpened the eye of the psychiatrist for factual data and made possible a method of description closely approximating to reality. But this apparently self-evident procedure is not, as it happens, self-evident at all, or rather, in no field of experience is the eye for facts so myopic as in the psyche's perception and observation of itself. Nowhere do prejudices, misinterpretations, value-judg-ments, idiosyncrasies, and projections trot themselves out more glibly and unashamedly than in this particular field of research, regardless of whether one is observing oneself or one's neigh-bour. Nowhere does the observer interfere more drastically with the experiment than in psychology. I am tempted to say that

one can never verify facts enough, because psychic experience is so extremely delicate and is moreover exposed to countless disturbing influences.

161   Nor should we omit to mention that whereas in all other departments of natural science a physical process is observed by a psychic process, in psychology the psyche observes itself, directly in the subject, indirectly in one's neighbour. One is reminded of the story of the topknot of Baron Munchausen, and consequently one comes to doubt whether psychological knowledge is possible at all. In this matter too the doctor feels grateful to natural science that he does not have to philosophize, but can enjoy living knowledge in and through the psyche. That is to say, although the psyche can never know anything *beyond* the psyche (that would be sheer Baron Munchausen!), it is still possible for two strangers to meet within the sphere of the psychic. They will never know themselves as they are, but only as they appear to one another. In the other natural sciences, the question of what a thing is can be answered by a knowledge that goes beyond the thing in question, namely by a psychic reconstruction of the physical process. But in what, or through what, can the psychic process be repeated? It can only be repeated in and through the psychic; in other words, there is no knowledge *about* the psyche, but only *in* the psyche.

162   Although, therefore, the medical psychologist mirrors the psychic in the psychic, he nevertheless remains, consistently with his empirical and phenomenological approach, within the framework of natural science; but at the same time he departs from it in principle in so far as he undertakes his reconstruction—knowledge and explanation—not in another medium, but in the same medium. Natural science combines two worlds, the physical and the psychic. Psychology does this only in so far as it is psychophysiology. As "pure" psychology its principle of explanation is *ignotum per ignotius,* for it can reconstruct the observed process only in the same medium from which that process is itself constituted. It is rather as if the physicist were unable to do anything except repeat the physical process in all its possible variations, without the aid of any *theoria.* But every psychic process, so far as it can be observed as such, is essentially *theoria,* that is to say, it is a *presentation;* and its reconstruction —or "re-presentation"—is at best only a variant of the same

87

presentation. If it is not that, it is just a compensatory attempt to improve or to find fault, or a piece of polemic or criticism; in either case it means the annulment of the process to be reconstructed. To adopt such a procedure in psychology is about as scientific as the paleontology of the eighteenth century, which interpreted *Andrias Scheuchzeri* (the giant salamander) as a human being who had been drowned in the Flood. This problem becomes acute when we have to do with contents which are difficult to understand, such as dream-images, manic ideas, and the like. Here the interpretation must guard against making use of any other viewpoints than those manifestly given by the content itself. If someone dreams of a lion, the correct interpretation can only lie in the direction of the lion; in other words, it will be essentially an *amplification* of this image. Anything else would be an inadequate and incorrect interpretation, since the image "lion" is a quite unmistakable and sufficiently positive presentation. When Freud asserts that the dream means something other than what it says, this interpretation is a "polemic" against the dream's natural and spontaneous presentation of itself, and is therefore invalid. A scientifically responsible interpretation which proceeds along the line of the image it wishes to interpret cannot be called a tautology; on the contrary, it enlarges the meaning of the image until it becomes, through amplification, a generally valid concept. Even a mathematical grasp of the psyche, were such a thing possible, could only be an algebraically expressed expansion of its meaning. Fechner's psychophysics is just the opposite of this, being an acrobatic attempt to jump over its own head.

163   At this crucial point psychology stands outside natural science. Although sharing with the latter its method of observation and the empirical verification of fact, it lacks the Archimedean point outside and hence the possibility of objective measurement. To that extent psychology is at a disadvantage compared with natural science. Only one other science finds itself in a similar situation, and that is atomic physics, where the process to be observed is modified by the observer. As physics has to relate its measurements to objects, it is obliged to distinguish the observing medium from the thing observed,[5] with the result that the categories of space, time, and causality become relative.

[5] I am indebted to Professor Markus Fierz, of Basel, for this formulation.

164   This strange encounter between atomic physics and psychology has the inestimable advantage of giving us at least a faint idea of a possible Archimedean point for psychology. The microphysical world of the atom exhibits certain features whose affinities with the psychic have impressed themselves even on the physicists.[6] Here, it would seem, is at least a suggestion of how the psychic process could be "reconstructed" in another medium, in that, namely, of the microphysics of matter. Certainly no one at present could give the remotest indication of what such a "reconstruction" would look like. Obviously it can only be undertaken by nature herself, or rather, we may suppose it to be happening continuously, all the time the psyche perceives the physical world. The case of psychology versus natural science is not altogether hopeless, even though, as said, the issue lies beyond the scope of our present understanding.

165   Psychology can also claim to be one of the humane sciences, or, as they are called in German, the *Geisteswissenschaften*, sciences of the mind. All these sciences of the mind move and have their being within the sphere of the psychic, if we use this term in its limited sense, as defined by natural science. From that point of view "mind" is a psychic phenomenon.[7] But, even as a science of the mind, psychology occupies an exceptional position. The sciences of law, history, philosophy, theology, etc., are all characterized and limited by their subject-matter. This constitutes a clearly defined mental field, which is itself, phenomenologically regarded, a psychic product. Psychology, on the other hand, though formerly counted a discipline of philosophy, is today a natural science and its subject-matter is not a mental product but a natural phenomenon, i.e., the psyche. As such it is among the elementary manifestations of organic nature, which

6 Cf. C. A. Meier's conspectus of the relevant literature, up to 1935, under "Moderne Physik—Moderne Psychologie," in *Die kulturelle Bedeutung der komplexen Psychologie* (Berlin, 1935), pp. 349ff. I would refer the reader particularly to the extensive quotations from articles by Niels Bohr, *Naturwissenschaft,* XVI (1928), 245, and XVII (1929), 483. Since the latter date see particularly Pascual Jordan, *Die Physik des 20. Jahrhunderts* (Brunswick, 1936), also his "Positivische Bemerkungen über die paraphysischen Erscheinungen," *Zentralblatt für Psychotherapie,* IX (1936), 3ff.; *Anschauliche Quantentheorie* (Berlin, 1936), pp. 271ff.; *Die Physik und das Geheimnis des organischen Lebens* (Brunswick, 1941), pp. 114ff.

7 Cf. my essay "Spirit and Life," *Coll. Works,* Vol. 8.

in turn forms one half of our world, the other half being the inorganic. Like all natural formations, the psyche is an irrational datum. It appears to be a special manifestation of life and to have this much in common with living organisms that, like them, it produces meaningful and purposeful structures with the help of which it propagates and continually develops itself. And just as life fills the whole earth with plant and animal forms, so the psyche creates an even vaster world, namely consciousness, which is the self-cognition of the universe.

166   In respect of its natural subject-matter and its method of procedure, modern empirical psychology belongs to the natural sciences, but in respect of its method of explanation it belongs to the humane sciences.[8] On account of this "ambiguity" or "double valence," doubts have been raised as to its scientific character, firstly on the score of this same ambivalence, secondly, on that of its alleged "arbitrariness." As to the latter point, it should not be forgotten that there are certain people who regard their psychic processes as purely arbitrary acts. They are naïvely convinced that everything they think, feel, want, and so on, is a product of their wills and is therefore "arbitrary." They believe that they think their own thoughts and want their own wants, there being no other subject of these activities except themselves. It is apparently impossible for them to admit that psychic activity could ever be carried on without a subject (in this case, of course, the ego). They balk at the idea that the psychic content, which they imagine they themselves have produced, exists in its own right, and is apparently far more the product of itself or of a will other than that of the ego.

167   Here we are up against a fashionable and widespread illusion in favour of the ego. In French they even go so far as to say "J'ai fait un rêve," although the dream is the one psychic content which least of all can be said to have been deliberately willed or created. Conversely, although German possesses the admirable expression "Einfall,"[9] nobody who "had a good idea" would feel the slightest compunction about chalking up this

8 Cf. Toni Wolff, "Einführung in die Grundlagen der komplexen Psychologie," Ch. I, *Die kulturelle Bedeutung der komplexen Psychologie.*
9 There are only pale reflections of this word in French and English, such as "idée," "idea," "sudden idea," etc. The German "witzige Einfall" fares a little better as "saillie" or "sally of wit" (from *saillir*, "to rush forth").

lucky fluke to his own account, as though it were something he had manufactured himself. But that, as the word "Einfall" clearly shows, is precisely not the case, firstly because of the obvious incapacity of the subject, and secondly because of the manifest spontaneity of the trans-subjective psyche. We therefore say in German, as well as in French and English, "The idea occurred to me," which is absolutely correct, seeing that the agent is not the subject but the idea, and that the idea literally dropped in through the roof.

168   These examples point to the objectivity of the psyche: it is a natural phenomenon and nothing "arbitrary." The will, too, is a phenomenon, though "free will" is not a natural phenomenon because it is not observable in itself, but only in the form of concepts, views, convictions, or beliefs. It is therefore a problem which belongs to a pure "science of the mind." Psychology has to confine itself to natural phenomenology if it is not to go poaching on other preserves. But the verification of the psyche's phenomenology is no simple matter, as we can see from this popular illusion concerning the "arbitrariness" of psychic processes.

169   As a matter of fact, there do exist psychic contents which are produced or caused by an antecedent act of the will, and which must therefore be regarded as products of some intentional, purposive, and conscious activity. To that extent a fair proportion of psychic contents are *mental* products. Yet the will itself, like the willing subject, is a phenomenon which rests on an unconscious background, where consciousness appears only as the intermittent functioning of an unconscious psyche. The ego, the subject of consciousness, comes into existence as a complex quantity which is constituted partly by the inherited disposition (character constituents) and partly by unconsciously acquired impressions and their attendant phenomena. The psyche itself, in relation to consciousness, is pre-existent and transcendent. We could therefore describe it, with du Prel,[10] as the transcendental subject.

170   Analytical psychology differs from experimental psychology in that it does not attempt to isolate individual functions (sense functions, emotional phenomena, thought-processes, etc.) and then subject them to experimental conditions for purposes of

10 Carl du Prel, *Das Rätsel des Menschen* (Leipzig, 1892), pp. 27ff.

investigation. It is far more concerned with the total manifestation of the psyche as a natural phenomenon—a highly complex structure, therefore, even though critical examination may be able to divide it up into simpler component complexes. But even these components are extremely complicated and, in their basic features, inscrutable. The boldness of our psychology in daring to operate with such unknowns would be presumptuous indeed, were it not that a higher necessity absolutely requires its existence and affords it help. We doctors are forced, for the sake of our patients, to treat obscure complaints which are hard or impossible to understand, sometimes with inadequate and therapeutically doubtful means, and to summon up the necessary courage and the right feeling of responsibility. We have, for professional reasons, to tackle the darkest and most desperate problems of the soul, conscious all the time of the possible consequences of a false step.

171   The difference between this and all earlier psychologies is that analytical psychology does not hesitate to tackle even the most difficult and complicated processes. Another difference lies in our method of procedure. We have no laboratory equipped with elaborate apparatus. Our laboratory is the world. Our tests are concerned with the actual, day-to-day happenings of human life, and the test-subjects are our patients, relatives, friends, and, last but not least, ourselves. Fate itself plays the role of experimenter. There are no needle-pricks, artificial shocks, surprise-lights, and all the paraphernalia of laboratory experiment; it is the hopes and fears, the pains and joys, the mistakes and achievements of real life that provide us with our material.

172   Our aim is the best possible understanding of life as we find it in the human soul. What we learn through understanding will not, I sincerely hope, petrify into intellectual theory, but will become an instrument which, through practical application, will improve in quality until it can serve its purpose as perfectly as possible. Its main purpose is the better adaptation of human behaviour, and adaptation in two directions (illness is faulty adaptation). The human being must be adapted on two fronts, firstly to external life—profession, family, society—and secondly to the vital demands of his own nature. Neglect of the one or the other imperative leads to illness. Although it is true that anyone whose unadaptedness reaches a certain point will eventually fall

ill, and will therefore also be a failure in life, yet not everybody is ill merely because he cannot meet the demands of the outside world, but rather because he does not know how to use his external adaptedness for the good of his most personal and intimate life and how to bring it to the right pitch of development. Some people become neurotic for external reasons, others for internal ones. It can easily be imagined how many different psychological formulations there must be in order to do justice to such diametrically opposite types. Our psychology inquires into the reasons for the pathogenic failure to adapt, following the slippery trail of neurotic thinking and feeling until it finds the way back to life. Our psychology is therefore an eminently practical science. It does not investigate for investigation's sake, but for the immediate purpose of giving help. We could even say that learning is its by-product, but not its principal aim, which is again a great difference from what one understands by "academic" science.

173   It is obvious that the purpose and inmost meaning of this new psychology is educational as well as medical. Since every individual is a new and unique combination of psychic elements, the investigation of truth must begin afresh with each case, for each "case" is individual and not derivable from any preconceived formula. Each individual is a new experiment of life in her ever-changing moods, and an attempt at a new solution or new adaptation. We miss the meaning of the individual psyche if we interpret it on the basis of any fixed theory, however fond of it we may be. For the doctor this means the individual study of every case; for the teacher, the individual study of every pupil. I do not mean that you should begin each investigation from the very bottom. What you already understand needs no investigating. I speak of "understanding" only when the patient or pupil can agree with the interpretations offered; understanding that goes over your patient's head is an unsafe business for both. It might be fairly successful with a child, but certainly not with an adult of any mental maturity. In any case of disagreement the doctor must be ready to drop all his arguments for the sole purpose of finding the truth. There are naturally cases where the doctor sees something which is undoubtedly there, but which the patient will not or cannot admit. As the truth is often hidden as much from the doctor as from the patient, various methods

have been evolved for gaining access to the unknown contents. I purposely say "unknown" and not "repressed" because I think it altogether wrong to assume that whenever a content is unknown it is necessarily repressed. The doctor who really thinks that way gives the appearance of knowing everything beforehand. Such a pretence stymies the patient and will most likely make it impossible for him to confess the truth. At all events the know-all attitude takes the wind out of his sails, though this is sometimes not altogether unwelcome to him, as he can then guard his secret the more easily, and it is so much more convenient to have his truth handed to him by the analyst than be forced to realize and confess it himself. In this way nobody is the gainer. Moreover, this superior knowing in advance undermines the patient's independence of mind, a most precious quality that should on no account be injured. One really cannot be careful enough, as people are incredibly eager to be rid of themselves, running after strange gods whenever occasion offers.

174   There are four methods of investigating the unknown in a patient.

175   The first and simplest method is the ASSOCIATION METHOD. I do not think I need go into details here, as this method has been known for the last fifty years. Its principle is to discover the main complexes through disturbances in the association experiment. As an introduction to analytical psychology and to the symptomatology of complexes, this method is recommended for every beginner.[11]

176   The second method, SYMPTOM-ANALYSIS, has a merely historical value and was given up by Freud, its originator, long ago. By means of hypnotic suggestion it was attempted to get the patient to reproduce the memories underlying certain pathological symptoms. The method works very well in all cases where a shock, a psychic injury, or a trauma is the chief cause of the neurosis. It was on this method that Freud based his earlier trauma theory of hysteria. But since most cases of hysteria are not of traumatic origin, this theory was soon discarded along with its method of investigation. In a case of shock the method can have a therapeutic effect through "abreaction" of the trau-

11 Cf. *Studies in Word Association, Coll. Works,* Vol. 2; and "A Review of the Complex Theory," *Coll. Works,* Vol. 8.

matic content. During and after the first World War it was useful in treating shell-shock and similar disorders.[12]

177   The third method, ANAMNESTIC ANALYSIS, is of greater importance as a method both of investigation and of therapy. In practice it consists in a careful anamnesis or reconstruction of the historical development of the neurosis. The material elicited in this way is a more or less coherent sequence of facts told to the doctor by the patient, so far as he can remember them. He naturally omits many details which either seem unimportant to him or which he has forgotten. The experienced analyst who knows the usual course of neurotic development will put questions which help the patient to fill in some of the gaps. Very often this procedure by itself is of great therapeutic value, as it enables the patient to understand the chief factors of his neurosis and may eventually bring him to a decisive change of attitude. It is of course as unavoidable as it is necessary for the doctor not only to ask questions, but to give hints and explanations in order to point out important connections of which the patient is unconscious. While serving as an officer in the Swiss Army Medical Corps, I often had occasion to use this anamnestic method. For instance, there was a nineteen-year-old recruit who reported sick. When I saw the young man he told me straight out that he was suffering from inflammation of the kidneys and that that was the cause of his pains. I wondered how he knew his diagnosis so definitely, whereupon he said that an uncle of his had the same trouble and the same pains in the back. The examination, however, revealed no trace of organic disease. It was obviously a neurosis. I asked for his previous history. The main fact was that the young man had lost both parents rather early and now lived with the uncle he had just mentioned. This uncle was his foster-father, of whom he was very fond. The day before he reported sick he received a letter from his uncle, telling him that he was laid up again with nephritis. The letter affected him unpleasantly and he threw it away at once, without realizing the true cause of the emotion he was trying to repress. Actually, he was very much afraid lest his foster-father should die, and this put him in mind again of his grief at the loss of his parents. As soon as he realized this he had a violent fit of weeping, with the result that he joined the ranks again next morning. It was a case

[12] Cf. the classic work of Breuer and Freud, *Studien über Hysterie* (1895).

of identification with the uncle, which was uncovered by the anamnesis. The realization of his suppressed emotions had a therapeutic effect.

178   A similar case was that of another recruit, who for weeks before I saw him had been having medical treatment for stomach trouble. I suspected that he was neurotic. The anamnesis revealed that the trouble began when he heard the news that his aunt, who was like a mother to him, had to undergo an operation for cancer of the stomach. Here again the uncovering of the hidden connection had curative results. Simple cases of this kind are quite common, and are accessible to anamnestic analysis. In addition to the favourable effect produced by the realization of previously unconscious connections, it is usual for the doctor to give some good advice, or encouragement, or even a reproof.

179   This is the best practical method for the treatment of neurotic children. With children you cannot very well apply the method of dream-analysis, as it penetrates deep into the unconscious. In the majority of cases you have simply to clear away certain obstacles, and this can be done without much technical knowledge. Generally speaking, a child's neurosis would be a very simple matter were it not that there is an invariable connection between it and the wrong attitude of the parents. This complication buttresses the child's neurosis against all therapeutic intervention.

180   The fourth method is the ANALYSIS OF THE UNCONSCIOUS. Despite the fact that anamnestic analysis can reveal certain facts of which the patient is unconscious, it is not what Freud would have called "psychoanalysis." In reality there is a remarkable difference between the two methods. The anamnestic method, as I pointed out, deals with conscious contents, or with contents ready for reproduction, while the analysis of the unconscious only begins when the conscious material is exhausted. I beg to point out that I do not call this fourth method "psychoanalysis," as I wish to leave that term entirely to the Freudians. What they understand by psychoanalysis is no mere technique, but a method which is dogmatically bound up with and based upon Freud's sexual theory. When Freud publicly declared that psychoanalysis and his sexual theory were indissolubly wedded, I was obliged to strike out on a different path, as I was unable to

endorse his one-sided views. That is also the reason why I prefer to call this fourth method the analysis of the unconscious.

181   As I have emphasized above, this method can only be applied when the conscious contents are exhausted. By this I mean that analysis of the unconscious is possible only after all the conscious material has been properly examined and there is still no satisfactory explanation and solution of the conflict. The anamnestic method often serves as an introduction to the fourth method. By careful examination of his conscious mind you get to know your patient; you establish what the old hypnotists used to call "rapport." This personal contact is of prime importance, because it forms the only safe basis from which to tackle the unconscious. This is a factor that is frequently overlooked, and when it is neglected it may easily lead to all sorts of blunders. Even the most experienced judge of human psychology cannot possibly know the psyche of another individual, so he must depend upon goodwill, i.e., good contact with the patient, and trust him to tell the analyst when anything goes wrong. Very often misunderstandings occur right at the beginning of the treatment, sometimes through no fault of the doctor. Owing to the very nature of his neurosis, the patient will harbour all kinds of prejudices which are often the direct cause of his neurosis and help to keep it alive. If these misunderstandings are not thoroughly cleared up, they can easily leave behind them a feeling of resentment which reduces all your subsequent efforts to nothing. Of course, if you begin the analysis with a fixed belief in some theory which purports to know all about the nature of neurosis, you apparently make your task very much easier; but you are nevertheless in danger of riding roughshod over the real psychology of your patient and of disregarding his individuality. I have seen any number of cases where the cure was hindered by theoretical considerations. Without exception the failure was due to lack of contact. It is only the most scrupulous observation of this rule that can prevent unforeseen catastrophes. So long as you feel the human contact, the atmosphere of mutual confidence, there is no danger; and even if you have to face the terrors of insanity, or the shadowy menace of suicide, there is still that area of human faith, that certainty of understanding and of being understood, no matter how black the night. It is by no means easy to establish such a contact, and you cannot achieve it at all except

97

by a careful comparison of both points of view and by mutual freedom from prejudice. Mistrust on either side is a bad beginning, and so is the forcible breaking down of resistances through persuasion or other coercive measures. Even conscious suggestion as part of the analytical procedure is a mistake, because the patient's feeling of being free to make up his own mind must at all costs be preserved. Whenever I discover the slightest trace of mistrust or resistance I try to take it with the utmost seriousness so as to give the patient a chance to re-establish the contact. The patient should always have a firm foothold in his conscious relation to the doctor, who in his turn needs that contact if he is to be sufficiently informed about the actual state of the patient's consciousness. He needs this knowledge for very practical reasons. Without it, he would not be able to understand his patient's dreams correctly. Therefore, not only in the beginning, but during the whole course of an analysis the personal contact must be the main point of observation, because it alone can prevent extremely disagreeable and surprising discoveries, as well as fatal issues so far as is humanly possible. And not only that, it is above all else a means for correcting the false attitude of the patient, in such a way that he does not feel he is being persuaded against his will or actually outwitted.

182   I should like to give you an illustration of this. A young man of about thirty, obviously very clever and highly intellectual, came to see me, not, he said, for treatment, but only in order to ask one question. He produced a voluminous manuscript, which, so he said, contained the history and analysis of his case. He called it a compulsion neurosis—quite correctly, as I saw when I read the document. It was a sort of psychoanalytical autobiography, most intelligently worked out and showing really remarkable insight. It was a regular scientific treatise, based on wide reading and a thorough study of the literature. I congratulated him on his achievement and asked him what he had really come for. "Well," he said, "you have read what I have written. Can you tell me why, with all my insight, I am still as neurotic as ever? In theory I should be cured, as I have recalled even my earliest memories. I have read of many people who, with infinitely less insight than I have, were nevertheless cured. Why should I be an exception? Please tell me what it is I have overlooked or am still repressing." I told him I could not at the moment see

any reason why his really astonishing insight had not touched his neurosis. "But," I said, "allow me to ask you for a little more information about yourself personally." "With pleasure," he replied. So I went on: "You mention in your autobiography that you often spend the winter in Nice and the summer in St. Moritz. I take it that you are the son of wealthy parents?" "Oh, no," he said, "they are not wealthy at all." "Then no doubt you have made your money yourself?" "Oh, no," he replied, smiling. "But how is it then?" I asked with some hesitation. "Oh, that does not matter," he said, "I got the money from a woman, she is thirty-six, a teacher in a council school." And he added, "It's a liaison, you know." As a matter of fact this woman, who was a few years older than himself, lived in very modest circumstances on her meagre earnings as a teacher. She saved the money by stinting herself, naturally in the hope of a later marriage, which this delightful gentleman was not even remotely contemplating. "Don't you think," I asked, "that the fact that you are financially supported by this poor woman might be one of the chief reasons why you are not yet cured?" But he laughed at what he called my absurd moral innuendo, which according to him had nothing to do with the scientific structure of his neurosis. "Moreover," he said, "I have discussed this point with her, and we are both agreed that it is of no importance." "So you think that by the mere fact of having discussed this situation you have talked the other fact—the fact of your being supported by a poor woman—out of existence? Do you imagine you have any lawful right to the money jingling in your pockets?" Whereupon he rose and indignantly left the room, muttering something about moral prejudices. He was one of the many who believe that morals have nothing to do with neurosis and that sinning on purpose is not sinning at all, because it can be intellectualized out of existence.

183   Obviously I had to tell this young gentleman what I thought of him. If we could have reached agreement on this point, treatment would have been possible. But if we had begun our work by ignoring the impossible basis of his life, it would have been useless. With views like his only a criminal can adapt to life. But this patient was not really a criminal, only a so-called intellectual who believed so much in the power of reason that he even thought he could unthink a wrong he had committed. I believe

99

firmly in the power and dignity of the intellect, but only if it does not violate the feeling-values. These are not just infantile resistances. This example shows what a decisive factor the personal contact is.

184 When the anamnestic stage of analysis is over, that is, when all the conscious material—recollections, questions, doubts, conscious resistances, etc—has been sufficiently dealt with, one can then proceed to the analysis of the unconscious. With this, one enters a new sphere. From now on we are concerned with the living psychic process itself, namely with DREAMS.

185 Dreams are neither mere reproductions of memories nor abstractions from experience. They are the undisguised manifestations of unconscious creative activity. As against Freud's view that dreams are wish-fulfilments, my experience of dreams leads me to think of them as functions of compensation. When, in the course of analysis, the discussion of conscious material comes to an end, previously unconscious potentialities begin to become activated, and these may easily be productive of dreams. Let me give an example. An elderly lady of fifty-four, but comparatively well preserved, came to consult me about her neurosis, which had begun about one year after the death of her husband twelve years before. She suffered from numerous phobias. Naturally she had a long story to unfold of which I will only mention the fact that, after the death of her husband, she lived by herself in her beautiful country house. Her only daughter was married and lived abroad. The patient was a woman of superficial education only, with a narrow mental horizon, who had learnt nothing in the last forty years. Her ideals and convictions belonged to the eighteen-seventies. She was a loyal widow and clung to her marriage as best she could without her husband. She could not understand in the least what the reason for her phobias could be; certainly it was no question of morals, as she was a worthy member of the church. Such people believe as a rule only in physical causes: phobias have regularly to do with the "heart," or the "lungs," or the "stomach." But strangely enough the doctors had found nothing wrong with those organs. Now she no longer knew what to think about her illness. So I told her that henceforth we would try to see what her dreams had to say on the question of her phobias. Her dreams at that time had the character of snapshots: a gramophone playing a love-song; herself as

a young girl, just engaged; her husband as a doctor, and so on. It was quite obvious what they were hinting at. In discussing the problem I was very careful not to call such dreams "wish-fulfilments," as she was already far too much inclined to say of her dreams, "Oh, they are nothing but fancies, one dreams such foolish stuff sometimes!" It was very important that she should give serious attention to this problem and feel that it really did concern her. The dreams contained her real intentions, and had to be added to the other contents of consciousness in order to compensate her blind one-sidedness. I call dreams compensatory because they contain ideas, feelings, and thoughts whose absence from consciousness leaves a blank which is filled with fear instead of with understanding. She wished to know nothing about the meaning of her dreams, because she felt it was pointless to think about a question which could not be answered at once. But, like many other people, she failed to notice that by repressing disagreeable thoughts she created something like a psychic vacuum which, as usually happens, gradually became filled with anxiety. Had she troubled herself consciously with her thoughts she would have known what was lacking, and she would then have needed no anxiety states as a substitute for the absence of conscious suffering.

186   Clearly, then, the doctor must know the conscious standpoint of his patient if he wants to have a secure basis for understanding the compensatory intention of dreams.

187   Experience tells us that the meaning and content of dreams are closely related to the conscious attitude. Recurrent dreams correspond to equally recurrent conscious attitudes. In the case just given it is easy to see what the dreams meant. But suppose a young girl, newly engaged, had such dreams: it is certain that they would have quite a different meaning. The analyst, therefore, must have a very good knowledge of the conscious situation, because it may happen that the same dream-motifs mean one thing on one occasion and the exact opposite on another. It is practically impossible, and it is certainly not desirable, to interpret dreams without being personally acquainted with the dreamer. Sometimes, however, one comes across fairly intelligible dreams, particularly with people who know nothing about psychology, where personal knowledge of the dreamer is not necessary for interpretation. Once, on a train journey, I

found myself with two strangers in the dining car. The one was a fine-looking old gentleman, the other a middle-aged man with an intelligent face. I gathered from their conversation that they were military men, presumably an old general and his adjutant. After a long silence, the old man suddenly said to his companion, "Isn't it odd what you dream sometimes? I had a remarkable dream last night. I dreamed *I was on parade with a number of young officers, and our commander-in-chief was inspecting us. Eventually he came to me, but instead of asking a technical question he demanded a definition of the beautiful. I tried in vain to find a satisfactory answer, and felt most dreadfully ashamed when he passed on to the next man, a very young major, and asked him the same question. This fellow came out with a damned good answer, just the one I would have given if only I could have found it.* This gave me such a shock that I woke up." Then, suddenly and unexpectedly addressing me, a total stranger, he asked, "D'you think dreams can have a meaning?" "Well," I said, "some dreams certainly have a meaning." "But what could be the meaning of a dream like that?" he asked sharply, with a nervous twitch of the face. I said, "Did you notice anything peculiar about this young major? What did he look like?" "He looked like me, when I was a young major." "Well, then," I said, "it looks as if you had forgotten or lost something which you were still able to do when you were a young major. Evidently the dream was calling your attention to it." He thought for a while, and then he burst out, "That's it, you've got it! When I was a young major I was interested in art. But later this interest got swamped by routine." Thereupon he relapsed into silence, and not a word more was spoken. After dinner I had an opportunity of speaking with the man whom I took to be his adjutant. He confirmed my surmise about the old gentleman's rank, and told me that I had obviously touched on a sore spot, because the general was known and feared as a crusty old disciplinarian who meddled with the most trifling matters that were no concern of his.

188   For the general attitude of this man it would certainly have been better if he had kept and cultivated a few outside interests instead of letting himself be drowned in mere routine, which was neither in his own interest nor in that of his work.

189   Had the analysis been carried further, I could have shown

him that he would be well advised to accept the standpoint of the dream. He would thus have been able to realize his one-sidedness, and correct it. Dreams are of inestimable value in this respect, provided that you keep away from all theoretical assumptions, as they only arouse unnecessary resistances in the patient. One such theoretical assumption is the idea that dreams are always repressed wish-fulfilments, generally of an erotic nature. It is far better, in actual practice, not to make any assumptions at all, not even that dreams must of necessity be compensatory. The fewer assumptions you have, and the more you can allow yourself to be acted upon by the dream and by what the dreamer has to say about it, the more easily you will arrive at the meaning of the dream. There are sexual dreams, just as there are hunger dreams, fever dreams, anxiety dreams, and others of a somatogenic nature. Dreams of this kind are clear enough, and no elaborate work of interpretation is needed to uncover their instinctual basis. So, guided by long experience, I now proceed on the principle that a dream expresses exactly what it means, and that any interpretation which yields a meaning not expressed in the manifest dream-image is therefore wrong. Dreams are neither deliberate nor arbitrary fabrications; they are natural phenomena which are nothing other than what they pretend to be. They do not deceive, they do not lie, they do not distort or disguise, but naïvely announce what they are and what they mean. They are irritating and misleading only because we do not understand them. They employ no artifices in order to conceal something, but inform us of their content as plainly as possible in their own way. We can also see what it is that makes them so strange and so difficult: for we have learned from experience that they are invariably seeking to express something that the ego does not know and does not understand. Their inability to express themselves more plainly corresponds to the inability, or unwillingness, of the conscious mind to understand the point in question. To take an example: if only our friend the general had taken the necessary time off from his undoubtedly exhausting duties to consider what it was that prompted him to go poking about in his soldiers' knapsacks—an occupation he would have done better to leave to his subordinates—he would have discovered the reason for his irritability and bad moods, and would thus have spared himself the annoying blow which my innocent interpretation dealt him. He could, with a little reflection, have understood the dream himself, for it was as simple and clear as could be wished. But it had the nasty quality of touching him on his blind spot; indeed it is this blind spot that spoke in the dream.

190   There is no denying that dreams often confront the psychologist with difficult problems, so difficult, indeed, that many psychologists prefer to ignore them, and to echo the lay prejudice that dreams are nonsense. But, just as a mineralogist would be ill advised to throw away his specimens because they are only worthless pebbles, so the psychologist and doctor denies himself the profoundest insight into the psychic life of his clients if he is prejudiced and ignorant enough to gloss over the utterances of the unconscious, not to speak of solving the scientific task which dreams impose on the investigator.

191   Since dreams are not pathological but quite normal phenomena, dream psychology is not the prerogative of the doctor but of psychologists in general. In practice, however, it is chiefly the doctor who will have to concern himself with dreams, because their interpretation offers the key to the unconscious. This key is needed above all by the doctor who has to treat neurotic and psychotic disorders. Sick people have a naturally stronger incentive to probe into their unconscious than have healthy people, and they therefore enjoy an advantage which the others do not share. It is very rare for the normal adult to find that an important part of his education has been neglected, and then to spend a large amount of time and money on getting a deeper insight into himself and a broader equability. As a matter of fact, so very much is lacking to the educated man of today that it is sometimes hard to tell him apart from a neurotic. Besides cases of the latter sort, who obviously need medical attention, there are numerous others who could be helped just as much by a practical psychologist.

192   Treatment by dream-analysis is an eminently educational activity, whose basic principles and conclusions would be of the greatest assistance in curing the evils of our time. What a blessing it would be, for instance, if even a small percentage of the population could be acquainted with the fact that it simply does not pay to accuse others of the faults from which one suffers most of all oneself!

193   The material you have to work with in the analysis of the unconscious consists not only of dreams. There are products of the unconscious which are known as fantasies. These fantasies are either a sort of day-dreaming, or else they are rather like visions and inspirations. You can analyse them in the same way as dreams.

194   There are two principal methods of interpretation which can be applied according to the nature of the case. The first is the so-called reductive method. Its chief aim is to find out the instinctive impulses underlying the dream. Take as an example the dreams of the elderly lady I mentioned a short while back. In her case, certainly, it was most important that she should see and understand the instinctive facts. But in the case of the old general it would have been somewhat artificial to speak of repressed biological instincts, and it is highly unlikely that he was repressing his aesthetic interests. Rather, he drifted away from them through force of habit. In his case, dream-interpretation would have a *constructive* purpose, as we should try to add something to his conscious attitude, rounding it out as it were. His sinking into a routine corresponds to a certain indolence and inertia which is characteristic of the Old Adam in us. The dream was trying to scare him out of it. But in the case of the elderly lady the understanding of the erotic factor would enable her consciously to recognize her primitive female nature, which for her is more important than the illusion of improbable innocence and strait-laced respectability.

195   Thus we apply a largely reductive point of view in all cases where it is a question of illusions, fictions, and exaggerated attitudes. On the other hand, a constructive point of view must be considered for all cases where the conscious attitude is more or less normal, but capable of greater development and refinement, or where unconscious tendencies, also capable of development, are being misunderstood and kept under by the conscious mind. The reductive standpoint is the distinguishing feature of Freudian interpretation. It always leads back to the primitive and elementary. The constructive standpoint, on the other hand, tries to synthesize, to build up, to direct one's gaze forwards. It is less pessimistic than the other, which is always on the look-out for the morbid and thus tries to break down something complicated into something simple. It may occasionally be necessary for

the treatment to destroy pathological structures; but treatment consists just as often, or even oftener, in strengthening and protecting what is healthy and worth preserving, so as to deprive the morbidities of any foothold. You can, if you like, regard not only every dream, but every symptom of illness, every characteristic, every manifestation of life from the reductive point of view, and thus arrive at the possibility of a negative judgment. If you go far enough back in your investigations, then we are all descended from thieves and murderers, and it is easy to show how all humility is rooted in spiritual pride, and every virtue in its corresponding vice. Which point of view he shall decide to adopt in any given case must be left to the insight and experience of the analyst. He will avail himself now of the one and now of the other in accordance with his knowledge of the character and conscious situation of his patient.

196   A few words on the symbolism of dreams and fantasies may not be out of place in this connection. Symbolism has today assumed the proportions of a science and can no longer make do with more or less fanciful sexual interpretations. Elsewhere I have attempted to put symbolism on the only possible scientific foundation, namely that of comparative research.[13] This method seems to have yielded extremely significant results.

197   Dream-symbolism has first of all a personal character which can be elucidated by the dreamer's associations. An interpretation that goes over the dreamer's head is not to be recommended, though it is perfectly possible in the case of certain symbolisms.[14] In order to establish the exact meaning which a dream has for the dreamer personally, the dreamer's collaboration is absolutely essential. Dream-images are many-faceted and one can never be sure that they have the same meaning in another dream or in another dreamer. A relative constancy of meaning is exhibited only by the so-called *archetypal* images.[15]

198   For the practical work of dream-analysis one needs a special knack and intuitive understanding on the one hand, and a con-

13 Cf. my *Symbols of Transformation, Coll. Works,* Vol. 5; "The Psychology of the Child Archetype" and "The Psychological Aspects of the Kore," *Coll. Works,* Vol. 9.
14 Cf. my "Individual Dream Symbolism in Relation to Alchemy," in *Psychology and Alchemy, Coll. Works,* Vol. 12.
15 Cf. my "Archetypes of the Collective Unconscious," *Coll. Works,* Vol. 9.

siderable knowledge of the history of symbols on the other. As in all practical work with psychology, mere intellect is not enough; one also needs feeling, because otherwise the exceedingly important feeling-values of the dream are neglected. Without these, dream-analysis is impossible. As the dream is dreamed by the whole man, it follows that anyone who tries to interpret the dream must be engaged as a whole man too. "Ars totum requirit hominem," says an old alchemist. Understanding and knowledge there must be, but they should not set themselves up above the heart, which in its turn must not give way to sentiment. All in all, dream-interpretation is an art, like diagnosis, surgery, and therapeutics in general—difficult, but capable of being learned by those whose gift and destiny it is.

LECTURE THREE

199   Through the analysis and interpretation of dreams we try to understand the tendencies of the unconscious. When I say "tendencies of the unconscious" it sounds very like a personification, as though the unconscious were a conscious being with a will of its own. But from the scientific standpoint it is simply a *quality* of certain psychic phenomena. One cannot even say that there is a definite class of psychic phenomena which regularly and under all circumstances have the quality of being unconscious. Anything may be, or become, unconscious. Anything you forget, or anything from which you divert your attention until it is forgotten, falls into the unconscious. In brief, anything whose energy-tension drops below a certain level becomes subliminal. If, to your lost memories, you add the many subliminal perceptions, thoughts, and feelings, you will get some idea of what constitutes as it were the upper layers of the unconscious.

199a   Such is the material you have to deal with in the first part of a practical analysis. Some of these unconscious contents have the special quality of being actively repressed by the conscious mind. Through the more or less deliberate withdrawal of attention from certain conscious contents, and through active resistance to them, they are eventually expelled from consciousness. A continual mood of resistance keeps these contents artificially below the threshold of potential consciousness. This is a regular occurrence in hysteria. It is the beginning of the personality split which is one of the most conspicuous features of this illness. Despite the fact that repression also occurs in relatively normal individuals, the total loss of repressed memories is a pathological symptom. Repression, however, should be clearly distinguished from suppression. Whenever you want to switch your attention from something in order to concentrate it on something else, you have to suppress the previously existing contents of consciousness, because, if you cannot disregard them, you will not be able to change your object of interest. Normally you can go back to the suppressed contents any time you like; they are always recoverable. But if they resist recovery, it may be a case of repression. In that case there must be some interest somewhere which wants to forget. Suppression does not cause forgetting, but repression definitely does. There is of course a perfectly normal process of forgetting which has nothing to do with repression. Repression is an artificial loss of memory, a self-suggested amnesia. It is not, in my experience, justifiable to assume that the unconscious consists wholly or for the greater part of repressed material. Repression is an exceptional and abnormal process, and the most striking evidence of this is the loss of feeling-toned contents, which one might think would persist in consciousness and remain easily recoverable. It can have effects very similar to those produced by concussion and by other brain injuries (e.g., by poisoning), for these cause an equally striking loss of memory. But whereas in the latter case absolutely all memories of a certain period are affected, repression causes what is called a *systematic amnesia*, where only specific memories or groups of ideas are withdrawn from recollection. In such cases a certain attitude or tendency can be detected on the part of the conscious mind, a deliberate intention to avoid even the bare possibility of recollection, for the very good reason that it would be painful or disagreeable. The idea of repression is quite in place here. This phenomenon can be observed most easily in the association experiment, where certain stimulus words hit the feeling-toned complexes. When they are touched, lapses or falsifications of memory (amnesia or paramnesia) are very common occurrences. Generally the complexes have to do with unpleasant things which one would rather forget and of which one has no wish to be reminded. The complexes themselves are the result, as a rule, of painful experiences and impressions.

200   Unfortunately, this rule is subject to certain limitations. It sometimes happens that even important contents disappear from

consciousness without the slightest trace of repression. They vanish automatically, to the great distress of the person concerned and not at all on account of some conscious interest which has engineered the loss and rejoices over it. I am not speaking here of normal forgetting, which is only a natural lowering of energy-tension; I am thinking rather of cases where a motive, a word, image, or person, vanishes without trace from the memory, to reappear later at some important juncture. These are cases of what is called cryptomnesia. (One such case, which concerned Nietzsche, is described in my "Psychology and Pathology of So-called Occult Phenomena," 1902.[1]) I remember, for instance, meeting a writer who later described our conversation in great detail in his autobiography. But the *pièce de résistance* was missing, namely a little lecture I read him on the origin of certain psychic disturbances. This memory was not in his repertoire. It reappeared, however, most significantly in another of his books devoted to this subject. For, in the last resort, we are conditioned not only by the past, but by the future, which is sketched out in us long beforehand and gradually evolves out of us. This is especially the case with a creative person who does not at first see the wealth of possibilities within him, although they are all lying there ready. So it may easily happen that one of these still unconscious aptitudes is called awake by a "chance" remark or by some other incident, without the conscious mind knowing exactly what has awakened, or even that anything has awakened at all. Only after a comparatively long incubation period does the result hatch out. The initial cause or stimulus often remains permanently submerged. A content that is not yet conscious behaves exactly like an ordinary complex. It irradiates the conscious mind and causes the conscious contents associated with it either to become supercharged, so that they are retained in consciousness with remarkable tenacity, or else to do just the opposite, becoming liable to disappear suddenly, not through repression from above, but through attraction from below. One may even be led to the discovery of certain hitherto unconscious contents through the existence of what one might call "lacunae," or eclipses in consciousness. It is therefore well worth while to look a bit more closely when you have the vague feeling of having overlooked or forgotten something. Naturally, if you assume

[1] *Coll. Works*, Vol. 1.

that the unconscious consists mainly of repressions, you cannot imagine any creative activity in the unconscious, and you logically arrive at the conclusion that eclipses are nothing but secondary effects following a repression. You then find yourself on a steep slope. The explanation through repression is carried to inordinate lengths, and the creative element is completely disregarded. Causalism is exaggerated out of all proportion and the creation of culture is interpreted as a bogus substitute activity. This view is not only splenetic, it also devalues whatever good there is in culture. It then looks as if culture were only a long-drawn sigh over the loss of paradise, with all its infantilism, barbarity, and primitiveness. In truly neurotic manner it is suggested that a wicked patriarch in the dim past forbade infantile delights on pain of castration. Thus, somewhat too drastically and with too little psychological tact, the castration myth becomes the aetiological culture-myth. This leads on to a specious explanation of our present cultural "discontent," [2] and one is perpetually smelling out regrets for some lost paradise which one ought to have had. That the sojourn in this barbarous little kindergarten is considerably more discontenting and uncomfortable than any culture up to 1933 is a fact which the weary European has had ample opportunity to verify for himself during the last few years. I suspect that the "discontent" has very personal motivations. Also, one can easily throw dust into one's own eyes with theories. The theory of repressed infantile sexuality or of infantile traumata has served innumerable times in practice to divert one's attention from the actual reasons for the neurosis,[3] that is to say, from all the slacknesses, carelessnesses, callousnesses, greedinesses, spitefulnesses, and sundry other selfishnesses for whose explanation no complicated theories of sexual repression are needed. People should know that not only the neurotic, but everybody, naturally prefers (so long as he lacks insight) never to seek the causes of any inconvenience in himself, but to push them as far away from himself as possible in space and time. Otherwise he would run the risk of having to make a change for the better. Compared with this odious risk it

---

[2] [Cf. Freud's *Civilization and Its Discontents*, trans. by Joan Rivière (London, 1930).—EDITORS.]

[3] Cf. the above-mentioned case (pars. 182f.) of a young man who sunned himself on the Riviera and in the Engadine.

seems infinitely more advantageous either to put the blame on to somebody else, or, if the fault lies undeniably with oneself, at least to assume that it somehow arose of its own accord in early infancy. One cannot of course quite remember how, but if one could remember, then the entire neurosis would vanish on the spot. The efforts to remember give the appearance of strenuous activity, and furthermore have the advantage of being a beautiful red herring. For which reason it may seem eminently desirable, from this point of view also, to continue to hunt the trauma as long as possible.

201 This far from unwelcome argument requires no revision of the existing attitude and no discussion of present-day problems. There can of course be no doubt that many neuroses begin in childhood with traumatic experiences, and that nostalgic yearnings for the irresponsibilities of infancy are a daily temptation to certain patients. But it remains equally true that hysteria, for instance, is only too ready to manufacture traumatic experiences where these are lacking, so that the patient deceives both himself and the doctor. Moreover it still has to be explained why the same experience works traumatically with one child and not with another.

202 Naïveté is out of place in psychotherapy. The doctor, like the educator, must always keep his eyes open to the possibility of being consciously or unconsciously deceived, not merely by his patient, but above all by himself. The tendency to live in illusion and to believe in a fiction of oneself—in the good sense or in the bad—is almost insuperably great. The neurotic is one who falls victim to his own illusions. But anyone who is deceived, himself deceives. Everything can then serve the purposes of concealment and subterfuge. The psychotherapist should realize that so long as he believes in a theory and in a definite method he is likely to be fooled by certain cases, namely by those clever enough to select a safe hiding-place for themselves behind the trappings of the theory, and then to use the method so skilfully as to make the hiding-place undiscoverable.

203 Since there is no nag that cannot be ridden to death, all theories of neurosis and methods of treatment are a dubious affair. So I always find it cheering when businesslike physicians and fashionable consultants aver that they treat patients along the lines of "Adler," or of "Künkel," or of "Freud," or even of

"Jung." There simply is not and cannot be any such treatment, and even if there could be, one would be on the surest road to failure. When I treat Mr. X, I have of necessity to use method X, just as with Mrs. Z I have to use method Z. This means that the method of treatment is determined primarily by the nature of the case. All our psychological experiences, all points of view whatsoever, no matter from what theory they derive, may be of use on the right occasion. A doctrinal system like that of Freud or Adler consists on the one hand of technical rules, and on the other of the pet emotive ideas of its author. Still under the spell of the old pathology, which unconsciously regarded diseases as distinct "entia" in the Paracelsian sense,[3a] each of them thought it possible to describe a neurosis as if it presented a specific and clearly defined clinical picture. In the same way doctors still hoped to capture the essence of the neurosis with doctrinaire classifications and to express it in simple formulae. Such an endeavour was rewarding up to a point, but it only thrust all the unessential features of the neurosis to the forefront, and thus covered up the one aspect that is essential, namely the fact that this illness is always an intensely individual phenomenon. The real and effective treatment of neurosis is always individual, and for this reason the stubborn application of a particular theory or method must be characterized as basically wrong. If it has become evident anywhere that there are not so much illnesses as ill people, this is manifestly the case in neurosis. Here we meet with the most individual clinical pictures it is possible to imagine, and not only that, but we frequently find in the neuroses contents or components of personality which are far more characteristic of the patient as an individual than the somewhat colourless figure he is all too likely to cut in civilian life. Because the neuroses are so extraordinarily individualistic, their theoretical formulation is an impossibly difficult task, as it can only refer to the collective features, i.e., those common to many individuals. But that is precisely the least important thing about the illness, or rather, it is totally irrelevant. Apart from this difficulty there is something else to be considered, the fact, namely, that nearly every psychological principle, every truth

[3a] [Cf. Jung, "Paracelsus as a Spiritual Phenomenon," *Coll. Works*, Vol. 13; and Jolande Jacobi, ed., *Paracelsus: Selected Writings* (New York [Bollingen Series XXVII] and London, 1951), p. 324.—EDITORS.]

113

relating to the psyche, must, if it is to be made absolutely true, immediately be reversed. Thus one is neurotic because one has repressions or because one does not have repressions; because one's head is full of infantile sex fantasies or because one has no fantasies; because one is childishly unadapted to one's environment or because one is adapted too exclusively to the environment; because one does or because one does not live by the pleasure principle; because one is too unconscious or because one is too conscious; because one is selfish or because one exists too little as a self; and so on. These antinomies, which can be multiplied at will, show how difficult and thankless is the task of theory-building in psychology.

204   I myself have long discarded any uniform theory of neurosis, except for a few quite general points like dissociation, conflict, complex, regression, *abaissement du niveau mental,* which belong as it were to the stock-in-trade of neurosis. In other words, every neurosis is characterized by dissociation and conflict, contains complexes, and shows traces of regression and *abaissement.* These principles are not, in my experience, reversible. But even in the very common phenomenon of repression the antinomial principle is already at work, since the principle "The chief mechanism of neurosis lies in repression" must be reversed because instead of repression we often find its exact opposite, the *drawing away* of a content, its subtraction or abduction, which corresponds to the "loss of soul" so frequently observed among primitives.[4] "Loss of soul" is not due to repression but is clearly a species of seizure, and is therefore explained as sorcery. These phenomena, originally belonging to the realm of magic, have not by any means died out in so-called civilized people.

205   A general theory of neurosis is therefore a premature undertaking, because our grasp of the facts is still far from complete. Comparative research into the unconscious has only begun.

206   Prematurely conceived theories are not without their dangers. Thus the theory of repression, whose validity in a definite field of pathology is incontestable—up to the point where it has to be reversed!—has been extended to creative processes, and the creation of culture relegated to second place, as a mere ersatz

---

[4] Called *"gana* loss" in South America. [Spanish, *gana* = lit., "appetite," "desire." See Count Hermann Keyserling, *South-American Meditations,* trans. by Theresa Duerr (New York and London, 1932), pp. 158ff., on this usage in Buenos Aires.— EDITORS.]

114

product. At the same time the wholeness and healthiness of the creative function is seen in the murky light of neurosis, which is of course an undoubted product of repression in many cases. In this way creativity becomes indistinguishable from morbidity, and the creative individual immediately suspects himself of some kind of illness, while the neurotic has lately begun to believe that his neurosis is an art, or at least a source of art. These would-be artists, however, develop one characteristic symptom: they one and all shun psychology like the plague, because they are terrified that this monster will gobble up their so-called artistic ability. As if a whole army of psychologists could do anything against the power of a god! True productivity is a spring that can never be stopped up. Is there any trickery on earth which could have prevented Mozart or Beethoven from creating? Creative power is mightier than its possessor. If it is not so, then it is a feeble thing, and given favourable conditions will nourish an endearing talent, but no more. If, on the other hand, it is a neurosis, it often takes only a word or a look for the illusion to go up in smoke. Then the supposed poet can no longer write, and the painter's ideas become fewer and drearier than ever, and for all this psychology is to blame. I should be delighted if a knowledge of psychology did have this sanative effect and if it put an end to the neuroticism which makes contemporary art such an unenjoyable problem. Disease has never yet fostered creative work; on the contrary, it is the most formidable obstacle to creation. No breaking down of repressions can ever destroy true creativeness, just as no analysis can ever exhaust the unconscious.

207   The unconscious is the ever-creative mother of consciousness. Consciousness grows out of the unconscious in childhood, just as it did in primeval times when man became man. I have often been asked how the conscious arose from the unconscious. The only possible way to answer this is to infer, from present experience, certain events which lie hidden in the abyss of the past, beyond the reach of science. I do not know whether such an inference is permissible, but it may be that even in those remote times consciousness arose in much the same way as it arises today. There are two distinct ways in which consciousness arises. The one is a moment of high emotional tension, comparable to the scene in *Parsifal* where the hero, at the very moment of greatest temptation, suddenly realizes the meaning of Amfortas'

wound. The other way is a state of contemplation, in which ideas pass before the mind like dream-images. Suddenly there is a flash of association between two apparently disconnected and widely separated ideas, and this has the effect of releasing a latent tension. Such a moment often works like a revelation. In every case it seems to be the discharge of energy-tension, whether external or internal, which produces consciousness. Many, though not all, of the earliest memories of infancy still retain traces of these sudden flashes of consciousness. Like the records handed down from the dawn of history, some of them are remnants of real happenings, others are purely mythical; in other words, some were objective in origin, and some subjective. The latter are often extremely symbolical and of great importance for the subsequent psychic life of the individual. Most of the earliest impressions in life are soon forgotten and go to form the infantile layer of what I have called the PERSONAL UNCONSCIOUS. There are definite reasons for this division of the unconscious into two parts. The personal unconscious contains everything forgotten or repressed or otherwise subliminal that has been acquired by the individual consciously or unconsciously. This material has an unmistakably personal stamp. But you can also find other contents which bear hardly any trace of a personal quality, and which appear incredibly strange to the individual. Such contents are frequently found in insanity, where they contribute not a little to the confusion and disorientation of the patient. In the dreams of normal people, too, these strange contents may occasionally appear. When you analyse a neurotic and compare his unconscious material with that of a man suffering from schizophrenia, you are instantly aware of a striking difference. With the neurotic, the material produced is mainly of a personal origin. His thoughts and feelings revolve round his family and his social set, but in a case of insanity the personal sphere is often completely swamped by collective representations. The madman hears the voice of God speaking to him; in his visions he sees cosmic revolutions, and it is just as if a veil has been twitched away from a world of ideas and emotions hitherto concealed. He suddenly begins talking of spirits, demons, witchcraft, secret magical persecutions, and so forth. It is not difficult to guess what this world is: it is the world of the primitive, which remains profoundly unconscious so long as everything is going well, but rises to the surface when some fatality befalls the conscious mind. This impersonal layer of the psyche I have termed the COLLECTIVE UNCONSCIOUS—"collective" because it is not an individual acquisition but is rather the functioning of the inherited brain structure, which in its broad outlines is the same in all human beings, and in certain respects the same even in mammals. The inherited brain is the product of our ancestral life. It consists of the structural deposits or equivalents of psychic activities which were repeated innumerable times in the life of our ancestors. Conversely, it is at the same time the ever-existing a priori type and author of the corresponding activity. Far be it from me to decide which came first, the hen or the egg.

208   Our individual consciousness is a superstructure based on the collective unconscious, of whose existence it is normally quite unaware. The collective unconscious influences our dreams only occasionally, and whenever this happens, it produces strange and marvellous dreams remarkable for their beauty, or their demoniacal horror, or for their enigmatic wisdom—"big dreams," as certain primitives call them. People often hide such dreams as though they were precious secrets, and they are quite right to think them so. Dreams of this kind are enormously important for the individual's psychic balance. Often they go far beyond the limits of his mental horizon and stand out for years like spiritual landmarks, even though they may never be quite understood. It is a hopeless undertaking to interpret such dreams reductively, as their real value and meaning lie in themselves. They are spiritual experiences that defy any attempt at rationalization. In order to illustrate what I mean, I should like to tell you the dream of a young theological student.[4a] I do not know the dreamer myself, so my personal influence is ruled out. He dreamed *he was standing in the presence of a sublime hieratic figure called the "white magician," who was nevertheless clad in a long black robe. This magician had just ended a lengthy discourse with the words "And for that we require the help of the black magician." Then the door suddenly opened and another old man came in, the "black magician," who however was dressed in a white robe. He too looked noble and sublime. The black magician evidently wanted to speak with the white, but hesitated to do so in the presence*

[4a] [This case is also discussed in *Two Essays on Analytical Psychology, Coll. Works,* Vol. 7, par. 287.—EDITORS.]

of the dreamer. At that the white magician said, pointing to the dreamer, "Speak, he is an innocent." So the black magician began to relate a strange story of how he had found the lost keys of paradise and did not know how to use them. He had, he said, come to the white magician for an explanation of the secret of the keys. He told him that the king of the country in which he lived was looking for a suitable monument for himself. His subjects had chanced to dig up an old sarcophagus containing the mortal remains of a virgin. The king opened the sarcophagus, threw away the bones and had the sarcophagus buried again for later use. But no sooner had the bones seen the light of day, than the being to whom they had once belonged—the virgin—changed into a black horse that galloped off into the desert. The black magician pursued it across the sandy wastes and beyond, and there after many vicissitudes and difficulties he found the lost keys of paradise. That was the end of his story and also, unfortunately, of the dream.

209   I think a dream like this will help to make clear the difference between an ordinary, personal dream and the "big" dream. Anybody with an open mind can at once feel the significance of the dream and will agree with me that such dreams come from a "different level" from that of the dreams we dream every night. We touch here upon problems of vast import, and it is tempting to dwell on this subject for a while. Our dream should serve to illustrate the activity of the layers that lie below the personal unconscious. The manifest meaning of the dream takes on a quite special aspect when we consider that the dreamer was a young theologian. It is evident that the relativity of good and evil is being presented to him in a most impressive manner. It would therefore be advisable to probe him on this point, and it would be exceedingly interesting to learn what a theologian has to say about this eminently psychological question. Also the psychologist would be in the highest degree interested to see how a theologian would reconcile himself to the fact that the unconscious, while clearly distinguishing between the opposites, nevertheless recognizes their identity. It is hardly likely that a youthful theologian would consciously have thought of anything so heretical. Who, then, is the thinker of such thoughts? If we further consider that there are not a few dreams in which

mythological motifs appear, and that these motifs are absolutely unknown to the dreamer, then the question arises of where such material comes from, since he has never encountered it anywhere in his conscious life, and who or what it is that thinks such thoughts and clothes them in such imagery—thoughts which, moreover, go beyond the dreamer's own mental horizon.[5] In many dreams and in certain psychoses we frequently come across archetypal material, i.e., ideas and associations whose exact equivalents can be found in mythology. From these parallels I have drawn the conclusion that there is a layer of the unconscious which functions in exactly the same way as the archaic psyche that produced the myths.

210   Although dreams in which these mythological parallels appear are not uncommon, the emergence of the collective unconscious, as I have called this myth-like layer, is an unusual event which only takes place under special conditions. It appears in the dreams dreamt at important junctures in life. The earliest dreams of childhood, if we can still remember them, often contain the most astonishing mythologems; we also find the primordial images in poetry and in art generally, while religious experience and dogma are a mine of archetypal lore.

211   The collective unconscious is a problem that seldom enters into practical work with children: their problem lies mainly in adapting themselves to their surroundings. Indeed, their connection with the primordial unconsciousness must be severed, as its persistence would present a formidable obstacle to the development of consciousness, which is what they need more than anything else. But if I were discussing the psychology of people beyond middle life, I should have a good deal more to say about the significance of the collective unconscious. You should always bear in mind that our psychology varies not only according to the momentary predominance of certain instinctive impulses and certain complexes, but according to the individual's life phase. You should be careful, therefore, not to impute an adult's psychology to a child. You cannot treat a child as you would an adult. Above all, the work can never be as systematic as with

---

[5] I do not wish to give offence to the dreamer of the dream under discussion, whom I do not know personally; but I hardly think that a young man of twenty-two would be conscious of the problem broached by this dream, at least, not of its full extent.

adults. A real, systematic dream-analysis is hardly possible, because with children the unconscious should not be stressed unnecessarily: one can easily arouse an unwholesome curiosity, or induce an abnormal precociousness and self-consciousness, by going into psychological details which are of interest only to the adult. When you have to handle difficult children, it is better to keep your knowledge of psychology to yourself, as simplicity and common sense are what they need most.[6] Your analytical knowledge should serve your own attitude as an educator first of all, because it is a well-known fact that children have an almost uncanny instinct for the teacher's personal shortcomings. They know the false from the true far better than one likes to admit. Therefore the teacher should watch his own psychic condition, so that he can spot the source of the trouble when anything goes wrong with the children entrusted to his care. He himself may easily be the unconscious cause of evil. Naturally we must not be too naïve in this matter: there are people, doctors as well as teachers, who secretly believe that a person in authority has the right to behave just as he likes, and that it is up to the child to adapt as best he may, because sooner or later he will have to adapt to real life which will treat him no better. Such people are convinced at heart that the only thing that matters is material success, and that the only real and effective moral restraint is the policeman behind the penal code. Where unconditional adaptation to the powers of this world is accepted as the supreme principle of belief, it would of course be vain to expect psychological insight from a person in authority as a moral obligation. But anyone who professes a democratic view of the world cannot approve of such an authoritarian attitude, believing as he does in a fair distribution of burdens and advantages. It is not true that the educator is always the one who educates, and the child always the one to be educated. The educator, too, is a fallible human being, and the child he educates will reflect his failings. Therefore it is wise to be as clear-sighted as possible about one's subjective views, and particularly about one's faults. As a man is, so will be his ultimate truth, and so also his strongest effect on others.

[6] This is not to be identified with ignorance. In order to get at an infantile neurosis or a difficult child, sound knowledge is needed as well as all the other things.

212   The psychology of children's neuroses can only be described very inadequately in general systematic terms, for, with few exceptions, the unique or individual features are overwhelmingly preponderant, as is usually also the case with the neuroses of adults. Here as there diagnoses and classifications have little meaning when weighed against the individual peculiarity of each case. Instead of a general description I should like to give you some examples from case histories, which I owe to the friendly collaboration of my pupil Frances G. Wickes, formerly consulting psychologist at St. Agatha's School, New York City.[7]

213   The first case is that of a boy seven years old. He had been diagnosed as mentally defective. The boy showed lack of co-ordination in walking, squinted in one eye and had an impediment in his speech. He was given to sudden outbursts of temper, and would keep the house in an uproar with his wild rages, throwing things about and threatening to kill the family. He liked to tease and to show off. At school he bullied the other children; he could not read, or take his place in class with children of the same age. After he had been at school for about six months, the rages increased until there were several each day. He was a first child, had been happy and friendly enough up to the age of five and a half, but between three and four he developed night terrors. He was late in learning to talk. The tongue was found to be tied, and an operation was performed. He could still hardly articulate at five and a half, and it was then discovered that the ligaments had not been properly cut. This was remedied. When he was five, a small brother was born. At first he was delighted, but as the baby grew older he seemed at times to hate him. As soon as his little brother began to walk, which he did unusually early, our patient started his wild tempers. He would show great vindictiveness, alternating with moods of affection and remorse. As these rages seemed to be brought on by almost anything, no matter how trifling, nobody thought of jealousy. As the rages increased, so the night terrors abated. Intelligence tests showed unusual ability in thinking.

---

[7] Well known as the author of *The Inner World of Childhood* (New York and London, 1927), and of *The Inner World of Man* (New York, London, and Toronto, 1938; 2nd edn., 1948). I should like to recommend the first book in particular to parents and teachers. [See the second paper in this volume, an introduction to the German edition.—EDITORS.]

He was delighted at every success and became friendly when encouraged, but was irritable over failures. The parents were brought to understand that the rages were compensatory power manifestations which he developed on realizing his own impotence, firstly when he saw how his little brother was praised and admired for doing with perfect ease the very thing that was impossible for him, and then in having to compete on such unequal terms with the other children at school. While he had remained the only child, whose parents lavished special care on him because of his handicaps, he was happy; but when he tried to hold his own on such unequal terms he became like a wild animal trying to break the chain. The rages, which the mother said were apt to occur "when some little bit of a thing went wrong," were often found to be connected with the times when the little brother was made to show off his tricks before visitors.

214   The boy soon developed very good relations with the psychologist, whom he called his "friend." He began to talk to her without falling into his rages. He would not tell his dreams, but would indulge in bombastic fantasies about how he was going to kill everybody and cut off their heads with a great sword. One day he suddenly interrupted himself and said: "That's what I'll do. What do you think of that?" The psychologist laughed and answered, "I think just as you do—it's all bunk." Then she gave him a picture of Santa Claus which he had admired, saying, "You and Santa Claus and I know it's all bunk." His mother put the picture in the window for him to see, and the next day he caught sight of it in one of his rages. He calmed down at once and remarked, "Santa Claus, that's all bunk!" and promptly did what he had been told to do. He then began to see his rages as something he enjoyed and used for a definite purpose. He showed remarkable intelligence in discerning his real motives. His parents and teachers co-operated in praising his efforts and not merely his successes. He was made to feel his place as the "eldest son." Special attention was given to speech training. Gradually he learned to control his rages. For a time the old night terrors became more frequent as the rages subsided, but then they too diminished.

215   One cannot expect a disorder that began so early on the basis of organ inferiorities to be cured at once. It will take years to reach a complete adaptation. A strong feeling of inferiority is

obviously at the bottom of this neurosis. It is a clear case of Adlerian psychology, where the inferiority gives rise to a power complex. The symptomatology shows how the neurosis attempted to compensate the loss of efficiency.

216   The second case concerns a little girl about nine years old. She had run a subnormal temperature for three months and was unable to attend school. Otherwise she showed no special symptoms, except loss of appetite and increasing listlessness. The doctor could find no reason for this condition. The father and mother were both sure they had the child's full confidence, and that she was not worried or unhappy in any way. The mother finally admitted to the psychologist that she and her husband did not get on together, but said that they never discussed their difficulties in front of the child, who was completely unconscious of them. The mother wanted a divorce, but could not make up her mind to face the upheaval it would involve. So everything remained in mid air, and in the meantime the parents made no effort to solve any of the difficulties causing their unhappiness. Both of them had an unduly possessive attachment to the child, who in turn had a terrific father-complex. She slept in her father's room in a little bed next to his and got into his bed in the mornings. She gave the following dream:

"I went with Daddy to see Granny. Granny was in a big boat. She wanted me to kiss her and wanted to put her arms round me, but I was afraid of her. Daddy said, 'Well then, I'll kiss Granny!' I didn't want him to do it, as I was afraid something might happen to him. Then the boat moved off and I couldn't find anybody and I felt frightened."

217   Several times she had dreams about Granny. Once Granny was all mouth, wide open. Another time she dreamt of "a big snake, which came out from under my bed and played with me." She often spoke of the snake dream, and had one or two others like it. The dream about her Granny she told with reluctance, but then confessed that every time her father went away she was frightened he would never come back. She had sized up her parents' situation, and told the psychologist that she knew her mother did not like her father, but she did not want to talk about it, "because it would make them feel bad." When her father was away on business trips she was always

afraid he would leave them. She had also noticed that her mother was always happier then. The mother realized that she was no help to the child, but on the contrary only made her ill by leaving the situation unsolved. The parents had either to tackle their difficulties together and try to come to a real understanding, or, if this should prove impossible, decide to separate. Eventually, they chose the latter course, and explained the situation to the child. The mother had been convinced that a separation would harm the child, instead of which her health improved as soon as the real situation came out into the open. She was told that she would not be parted from either parent but would have two homes instead; and although a divided home seems a poor arrangement for any child, her relief at no longer being a prey to vague fears and forebodings was so great that she returned to normal health and to real enjoyment of school and play.

217a   A case like this is often a great puzzle to the general practitioner. He looks in vain for an organic cause of the trouble, not knowing that he ought to look elsewhere, for no medical textbook would admit the possibility that psychic difficulties between father and mother could be responsible for the child's subnormal temperature. But to the analyst such causes are by no means unknown or strange. The child is so much a part of the psychological atmosphere of the parents that secret and unsolved problems between them can influence its health profoundly. The *participation mystique,* or primitive identity, causes the child to feel the conflicts of the parents and to suffer from them as if they were its own. It is hardly ever the open conflict or the manifest difficulty that has such a poisonous effect, but almost always parental problems that have been kept hidden or allowed to become unconscious. The author of these neurotic disturbances is, without exception, the unconscious. Things that hang in the air and are vaguely felt by the child, the oppressive atmosphere of apprehension and foreboding, these slowly seep into the child's soul like a poisonous vapour.

218   What this child seemed to feel most was the unconscious of her father. If a man has no real relations with his wife, then obviously he seeks another outlet. And if he is not conscious of what he is seeking, or if he represses fantasies of that kind, his interest will regress on the one side to the memory-image of

his mother, and on the other side it invariably fastens on his daughter, if there is one. This is what might be called unconscious incest. You can hardly hold a man responsible for his unconsciousness, but the fact remains that in this matter nature knows neither patience nor pity, and takes her revenge directly or indirectly through illness and unlucky accidents of all kinds. Unfortunately, it is almost a collective ideal for men and women to be as unconscious as possible in the ticklish affairs of love. But behind the mask of respectability and faithfulness the full fury of neglected love falls upon the children. You cannot blame the ordinary individual, as you cannot expect people to know the attitude they ought to adopt and how they are to solve their love problems within the framework of present-day ideals and conventions. Mostly they know only the negative measures of negligence, procrastination, suppression, and repression. And to know of anything better is admittedly very difficult.

219   The dream about the grandmother shows how the unconscious psychology of the father is penetrating that of the child. It is he who wishes to kiss his mother, and the child feels forced to kiss her in the dream. The grandmother who is "all mouth" suggests swallowing and devouring.[8] Obviously the child is in danger of being swallowed by her father's regressive libido. That is why she dreams of the snake; for the snake, since ancient times, has always been the symbol of danger: of being caught in coils, or swallowed, or poisoned.[9] This case also shows how apt children are to see very much more than their parents suspect. It is of course not possible for parents to have no complexes at all. That would be superhuman. But they should at least come to terms with them consciously; they should make it a duty to work out their inner difficulties for the sake of the children. They should not take the easy road of repressing them in order to avoid painful discussions. The love problem is part of mankind's heavy toll of suffering, and nobody should be ashamed of having to pay his tribute. It is a thousand times

---

[8] This is the manifestation of an archetype, namely that of the deadly, devouring mother. Cf. the fairytales of Red Riding Hood and of Hansel and Gretel, and the South Sea myth of Maui and Hine-nui-te-po, the tribal ancestress who sleeps with her mouth open. Maui creeps into the mouth and is swallowed (Leo Frobenius, *Das Zeitalter des Sonnengottes*, Berlin, 1904, I, pp. 66ff.).

[9] Cf. the snake symbolism in *Symbols of Transformation, Coll. Works*, Vol. 5.

better in every respect for parents frankly to discuss their problems, instead of leaving their complexes to fester in the unconscious.

220   In a case like this, what would be the use of talking to the child about incestuous fantasies and father-fixations? Such a procedure would only make her believe that it was all the fault of her own immoral or foolish nature, and would burden her with a responsibility which is not hers at all, but really belongs to her parents. She suffers not because she has unconscious fantasies but because her father has them. She is a victim of the wrong atmosphere in the home, and her problem disappears as soon as her parents faced up to theirs.

221   The third case concerns a very intelligent girl of thirteen, reported as anti-social, rebellious, and unable to adapt herself to school conditions. At times she was very inattentive and would give peculiar answers for which she could offer no explanation. She was a big, well-developed girl, apparently in the best of health. She was several years younger than her classmates, trying, with her thirteen years, to lead the life of a young girl of sixteen or seventeen, but without the corresponding capabilities. Physically she was over-developed, puberty having begun when she was barely eleven. She was frightened of her sexual excitability and of her desire to masturbate. Her mother was a woman of brilliant intellect, with an intense will to power, who had early decided that her daughter must be a prodigy. She had forced every intellectual faculty and suppressed all emotional growth. She wanted the child to go to school earlier than anybody else. The father's business took him from home a good deal, and to the girl he seemed more like a shadowy ideal than an actual reality. She suffered from a tremendous pressure of pent-up emotions which fed more upon homosexual fantasies than upon real relationships. She confessed that she sometimes longed to be caressed by a certain teacher, and then suddenly she would fancy that all her clothes had dropped off, so that she lost track of what was being said to her; hence her absurd answers. This is one of her dreams: *"I saw my mother slipping down the bath and I knew she was drowning, but I could not move. Then I grew terribly frightened and started to weep because I had let her drown. I woke up crying."* This dream helped her to bring to the surface the hidden resistances to the un-

natural life she was forced to lead. She acknowledged her desire for normal companionship. Little could be done at home, but a change of surroundings, the understanding of her problem, and the frank discussion brought a considerable improvement.

222   This case is simple, but very typical. The role played by the parents is again most conspicuous. It was one of those typical marriages where the father is completely wrapped up in his business, and the mother tries to realize her social ambitions through the child. The child had to be a success in order to satisfy her mother's desires and expectations and to flatter her vanity. A mother like this does not as a rule see the real character of her child at all, or her individual ways and needs. She projects herself into the child and rules her with a ruthless will to power. Such a marriage is all too likely to produce just that psychological situation and to intensify it still further. There seems to have been a considerable distance between husband and wife, as so masculine a woman can hardly have had any real understanding of a man's feelings: the only thing she knows how to get out of him is his money. He pays her in order to keep her in a fairly tolerable mood. All her love turns into ambition and will to power (if indeed she has not been doing this since long before her marriage, unconsciously following the example of her own mother). The children of such mothers are practically nothing more than dolls, to be dressed up and adorned at pleasure. They are nothing but mute figures on the chessboard of their parents' egoism, and the maddening thing is that all this is done under the cloak of selfless devotion to the dear child, whose happiness is the sole aim of the mother's life. But in actual fact the child is not given a grain of real love. That is why she suffers from premature sexual symptoms, like so many other neglected and ill-treated children, while at the same time she is deluged with so-called maternal love. The homosexual fantasies clearly show that her need for real love is not satisfied; consequently she craves love from her teachers, but of the wrong sort. If tender feelings are thrown out at the door, then sex in violent form comes in through the window, for besides love and tenderness a child needs understanding. The right thing in this case would naturally be to treat the mother, which might do something to improve her marriage and deflect her passion from the child, at the same time giving the latter access to her mother's

heart. Failing that, one can only try to check the mother's injurious influence by stiffening the child's resistance to her, so that she will at least be able to criticize her mother's faults with fairness and become conscious of her own individual needs. Nothing is more stunting than the efforts of a mother to embody herself in her child, without ever considering that a child is not a mere appendage, but a new and individual creature, often furnished with a character which is not in the least like that of the parents and sometimes seems to be quite frighteningly alien. The reason for this is that children are only nominally descended from their parents, but are actually born from the ancestral stock. Occasionally you have to go back several hundred years to see the family likeness.

223   The child's dream is quite intelligible: it obviously means the death of the mother.[10] Such is the answer of the child's unconscious to the mother's blind ambition. Had she not tried to "kill" her daughter's individuality the unconscious would never have reacted in that way. Certainly you should never start generalizing from the results of such a dream. Death-dreams about the parents are not uncommon, and you might be led to suppose that they are always based on the kind of conditions I have just described. But you should remember that a dream-image does not always have the same meaning in all circumstances. You can never be certain of a dream's meaning unless you are sufficiently acquainted with the conscious situation of the dreamer.

224   The last case I shall mention concerns an eight-year-old girl, Margaret, who suffered from a complaint that does not seem to be causally connected with the parents. It is a complicated case which cannot be dealt with fully in a lecture. I have therefore selected only one important phase in its development. The child had been at school for a year without being able to learn anything, except a little reading. She moved clumsily, went up and down stairs like a child just beginning to walk, had little control of her limbs, and spoke in a whining voice. In conversation she would show intense eagerness at first, then suddenly bury her face in her hands and refuse to say any more. As soon as she

10 Superficially this dream can be understood as a wish-fulfilment, but closer examination would show that it sums up the facts. For the daughter the mother signifies the feminine instinctual ground-layer which in this case is profoundly disturbed.

started to speak she would burst into a weird gibberish made up of disconnected words. When she tried to write she drew single letters, and then covered the whole paper with scribbles which she called "funnies." Intelligence tests could not be given in the normal way, but in several thinking and feeling tests she got the results of an eleven-year-old, in others barely those of a child of four. She had never been normal. When she was ten days old, blood clots resulting from the difficult birth had to be removed from the cranial cavity. She was watched over day and night and looked after with the greatest care. It soon became apparent that she used her physical disabilities to tyrannize her parents, meanwhile resenting any attempt to help her. The parents tried to compensate her defects by shielding her from reality and by providing her with moral crutches which kept her from struggling to overcome her difficulties and frustrations through an effort of will.

225   The first psychological approach was through the world of imagination. As the child was fairly imaginative, she began to learn to read for the sake of stories, and, once started, she progressed with astonishing rapidity. Too much concentration on one thing made her irritable and excited, but nevertheless there was a steady gain. One day Margaret announced, "I have a twin sister. She is called Anna. She is just like me except that she always wears lovely pink clothes and has glasses. [Glasses meant her weak eyes, which kept her from poring over the books she now loved.] If Anna were here I should work better." The psychologist suggested that Anna should be asked to come in. Margaret went out into the hall and came back with Anna. Then she tried to write, so as to show Anna. After that, Anna was always present. First Margaret would write, then Anna. One day everything went wrong, and finally she burst out, "I shall never learn to write and it's all Mother's fault! I am left-handed, and she never told my first teacher. I had to try to write with my right hand, and now I shall grow up and never be able to write because of Mother." The psychologist told her of another child who was also left-handed and whose mother had made the same mistake. Margaret inquired eagerly, "So he can't write at all?" "Oh, no," said the psychologist, "he writes stories and all sorts of things, only it was harder for him, that's all. He generally writes with his left hand now. You can write with your

left hand if you want to." "But I like my right hand best." "Oho, then it doesn't seem to be all your mother's fault. I wonder whose fault it is?" Margaret only said, "I don't know." Thereupon it was suggested that she might ask Anna. So she went out and came back after a while and said, "Anna says it's my fault and I had better do some work." Before this she had always refused to discuss her responsibility, but from now on she would go out of the room, talk it over with Anna, and bring back the result. Sometimes she would come back with all the signs of rebellion, but she always told the truth. Once, after railing against Anna, she said, "But Anna insists, 'Margaret, it's your own fault. You've got to try.' " From this she went on to a realization of her own projections. One day she got into a fearful temper with her mother. She burst into the room, shouting, "Mother is horrid, horrid, horrid!" "Who is horrid?" she was asked. "Mother," she answered. "You might ask Anna," said the psychologist. There was a long pause, then she said, "Pooh! I guess I know as much as Anna. I'm horrid. I'll go and tell Mother." This she did and then returned quietly to her work.

226   As a result of the serious injury at birth the child had not been able to develop properly. She naturally deserved, and received, a good deal of attention from her parents; but it is almost impossible to draw the line and to know exactly how far one should go in considering a child's incapacities. Somewhere, certainly, the optimum is reached, and if you go beyond that you start spoiling the child. As the first-mentioned case shows, children do feel their inferiority in certain ways, and they begin to compensate by assuming a false superiority. This is only another inferiority, but a moral one; no genuine satisfaction results, and so a vicious circle is begun. The more a real inferiority is compensated by a false superiority, the less the initial inferiority is remedied, and the more it is intensified by the feeling of moral inferiority. This necessarily leads to more false superiority, and so on at an ever increasing rate. Obviously, Margaret needed a great deal of attention and was therefore involuntarily spoiled, so that she learnt to exploit the legitimate devotion of her parents. As a result, she got stuck in her incapacity and defeated her own efforts to extricate herself, remaining more incapable and more infantile than her actual handicaps warranted.

227   Such a condition is most favourable to the growth of a second personality. The fact that her conscious mind fails to progress does not mean in the least that her unconscious personality will also remain at a standstill. This part of herself will advance as time goes on, and the more the conscious part hangs back, the greater will be the dissociation of personality. Then one day the more developed personality will appear on the scene and challenge the regressive ego. This was the case with Margaret: she saw herself confronted by "Anna," her superior twin sister, who for a while represented her moral reason. Later the two merged into one, and this signified a tremendous advance. In 1902, I published a study of very much the same psychological structure. It was about a young girl of sixteen with a quite extraordinary dissociation of personality. You will find it in my paper on "The Psychology and Pathology of So-called Occult Phenomena." [11] The educational use which the psychologist made of the second personality brought excellent results, and entirely agreed with the teleological significance of the figure of Anna. The psychic double is a commoner phenomenon than one would expect, although it seldom reaches a degree of intensity that would entitle one to speak of a "double personality."

* * *

228   About education in general and school education in particular the doctor has little to say from the standpoint of his science, as that is hardly his business. But on the education of difficult or otherwise exceptional children he has an important word to add. He knows only too well from his practical experience what a vital role parental influences and the effects of schooling play even in the life of the adult. He is therefore inclined, when dealing with children's neuroses, to seek the root cause less in the child itself than in its adult surroundings, and more particularly in the parents. Parents have the strongest effect upon the child not only through its inherited constitution, but also through the tremendous psychic influence they themselves exert. That being so, the uneducatedness and unconsciousness of the adult works far more powerfully than any amount of good advice, commands, punishments, and good intentions. But when, as is unfortunately all too often the case, parents and teachers

11 *Coll. Works,* Vol. 1.

expect the child to make a better job of what they themselves do badly, the effect is positively devastating. Again and again we see parents thrusting their unfulfilled illusions and ambitions on to the child, and forcing it into a role for which it is in no circumstances fitted. I remember being consulted about a badly behaved little boy. From the parents' account I learnt that, at the age of seven, he could neither read nor write, that he would not learn any of his lessons properly, resisting, with unreasoning defiance, every attempt to educate him, and that for two years he had been developing rages in which he smashed everything within reach. He was intelligent enough, so the parents thought, but totally lacking in goodwill. Instead of working he lazed about or played with his decrepit old Teddy bear, which for years had been his only toy. He had been given plenty of other toys, but he viciously destroyed them. They had even engaged a good governess for him, but she could do nothing with him either. He was, after a couple of girls, the first and only son, on whom, so it seemed to me, the mother doted especially. As soon as I saw the child the riddle was solved: the boy was pretty much of an imbecile already, and the mother, who could not endure having a backward son, had so egged on and tormented this essentially harmless and good-natured zany with her ambitions that he went completely berserk out of sheer desperation. When I spoke to the mother after the examination she was outraged by my diagnosis and insisted that I must have made a mistake.

229   The educator should know above all else that talk and officious discipline lead nowhere, that what counts is example. If he unconsciously permits all kinds of viciousness, lies, and bad manners in himself, these will have an incomparably more powerful effect than the best of intentions, which are so easily come by. The doctor therefore believes that the best way to educate others is for the educator himself to be educated, and that he should first try out on himself the psychological profundities he has learnt from text-books, in order to test their efficacy. So long as these efforts are prosecuted with a certain amount of intelligence and patience, he will probably not make such a bad teacher.

V

THE GIFTED CHILD

THE GIFTED CHILD [1]

230   When I visited the United States for the first time, I was
much astonished to see that there were no barriers at the railway
crossings and no protective hedges alongside the railway track.
In the remoter districts the line was actually used as a foot-path.
When I voiced my astonishment about this, I was informed,
"Only an idiot could fail to see that trains pass along the line at
forty to a hundred miles an hour!" Another thing that struck
me was that nothing is *verboten;* instead, one is merely "not
allowed" to do something, or one is politely requested: "Please
don't———."

231   These impressions, and others like them, reduced themselves
to the discovery that in America civic life appeals to the intelligence and expects an intelligent response, whereas in Europe
it plans for stupidity. America fosters and looks forward to intelligence; Europe looks back to see whether the dumb ones
are also coming along. What is worse, Europe takes evil intentions for granted and is forever crying that bossy and officious
"Verboten!" into our ears, whereas America addresses herself
to people's common sense and goodwill.

1 [This was first delivered at the annual meeting of the Basel School Council, in
December, 1942. It was published as "Der Begabte" in the *Schweizer Erziehungs-
Rundschau,* XVI (1943): 1, and in *Psychologie und Erziehung* (Zurich, 1946), from
which the present translation is made.—EDITORS.]

232   Involuntarily I found my thoughts drifting back to my school-days, and there I saw the European prejudice embodied in certain of my teachers. I was not, as a twelve-year-old school-boy, by any means drowsy or stupid, but often I felt uncommonly bored when the teacher had to busy himself with the slowcoaches. I had the good fortune to possess a genial Latin master who, during the exercises, used to send me to fetch books from the university library, and in these I browsed with delight as I dawdled back by the longest possible route. Boredom, however, was by no means the worst of my experiences. Once, among the numerous and not exactly stimulating themes for an essay, we were given something really interesting. I set to work very seriously and polished my sentences with the greatest care. In happy anticipation of having written the best, or at least one of the better essays, I handed mine in to the teacher. When giving them back he always used to discuss the best essay first, and then the others in order of merit. All the others came before mine, and when the last, feeblest effort was about to be discussed, the teacher inflated himself in a manner that boded disaster, and pronounced the following words: "Jung's essay is by far the best, but he has composed it frivolously and dashed it off without taking any trouble. Therefore it merits no attention whatever." "That is not true," I cried, "I've never put so much work into any essay as I did into this." "That's a lie!" he shouted. "Look at Smith Minor"—the boy who had produced the worst essay—"*he* took trouble over his. He will get on in life, but you won't, no, not you—for in life you can't get away with cleverness and humbug." I was silent. From that moment I never did a stroke of work during German lessons.

233   This mishap lies more than half a century behind me, and I have no doubt that there have been many changes and improvements in the school since then. But, at the time, it obsessed my thoughts and left me with a feeling of bitterness, though this naturally gave place to better understanding as my experience of life increased. I came to realize that my teacher's attitude was after all based on the noble precept of helping the weak and eradicating the bad. But, as so often happens with such precepts, they are apt to be elevated to soulless principles which do not bear thinking about further, so that a lamentable caricature of goodness results: one helps the weak and fights against the bad,

but at the same time one runs the risk of putting the gifted child in a back place, as though being ahead of one's fellows were something scandalous and improper. The average person distrusts and readily suspects anything that his intelligence cannot grasp. *Il est trop intelligent*—reason enough for the blackest suspicion! In one of his novels Paul Bourget describes an exquisite scene in the antechamber of some Minister, which serves as the perfect paradigm. A middle-class couple offer this criticism of a celebrated scholar, with whom of course they are not acquainted: "Il doit être de la police secrète, il a l'air si méchant."

234   I trust you will forgive me for having dwelt so long on autobiographical details. Nevertheless this *Wahrheit* without the *Dichtung* is not just an isolated instance; it is something that happens all too often. The gifted schoolchild faces us with an important task which we cannot ignore, despite that worthy maxim about helping the less gifted. In a country as small as Switzerland we cannot afford, however charitable our aspirations may be, to overlook these much-needed gifted children. Even today we seem to proceed somewhat diffidently in this matter. Not long ago I heard of the following case: An intelligent little girl in one of the lower forms at a primary school suddenly became a bad pupil, much to the astonishment of her parents. The things the child said out of school sounded so comical that her parents got the impression that the children were treated like idiots and were being stultified artificially. So the mother went to see the Principal about it and discovered that the teacher had been trained to cope with defectives and had formerly looked after backward children. Obviously she did not know the first thing about normal ones. Luckily the damage was caught in time, so that the child could be passed on to a normal teacher under whom she soon picked up again.

235   The problem of the gifted child is not at all simple, because he is not distinguished merely by the fact of being a good pupil. Occasionally he is the exact opposite. He may even be notoriously absent-minded, have his head full of other things, be indolent, slovenly, inattentive, badly behaved, self-willed, or evoke the impression of being half asleep. From external observation alone it is sometimes difficult to distinguish the gifted child from a mental defective.

236   Nor should we forget that gifted children are not always precocious, but may on the contrary develop slowly, so that the gift remains latent for a long time. The giftedness can then be spotted only with difficulty. On the other hand too much good-will and optimism on the part of the teacher can imagine talents that later turn out to be blanks, as in the biography which says: "No signs of genius were observable up to his fortieth year—nor indeed afterwards."

237   Sometimes the only thing that helps in diagnosing a gift is careful observation of the child's individuality both in school and at home, which alone enables us to see what is primary disposition and what is secondary reaction. In the gifted child inattentiveness, absent-mindedness, and day-dreaming may prove to be a secondary defence against outside influences, in order that the interior fantasy processes may be pursued undisturbed. Admittedly the mere existence of lively fantasies or peculiar interests is no proof of special gifts, as the same predominance of aimless fantasies and abnormal interests may also be found in the previous history of neurotics and psychotics. What does reveal the gift, however, is the *nature* of these fantasies. For this one must be able to distinguish an intelligent fantasy from a stupid one. A good criterion of judgment is the originality, consistency, intensity, and subtlety of the fantasy structure, as well as the latent possibility of its realization. One must also consider how far the fantasy extends into the child's actual life, for instance in the form of hobbies systematically pursued and other interests. Another important indication is the degree and quality of his interest in general. One sometimes makes surprising discoveries where problem children are concerned, such as a voracious and apparently indiscriminate reading of books, done mostly in the forbidden hours after bedtime, or else some unusual practical accomplishment. All these signs can only be understood by one who takes the trouble to inquire into the reasons for the child's problems, and who is not content merely to pick on the bad qualities. A certain knowledge of psychology —by which I mean common sense and experience—is therefore a desirable requisite in a teacher.

238   The psychic disposition of the gifted child always moves in violent contrasts. That is to say, it is extremely rare for the gift to affect all regions of the psyche uniformly. The general rule is

that one or the other region will be so little developed as to entitle us to speak of a defect. Above all the degree of maturity
differs enormously. In the region of the gift abnormal precocity
may prevail, while outside that region the mental attainment
may be below normal for a child of that age. Occasionally this
gives rise to a misleading picture: one thinks one is dealing with
a rather undeveloped and mentally backward child and, in consequence, fails to credit him with any ability above the normal.
Or it may be that a precocious intellect is not accompanied by
a corresponding development of verbal facility, so that the child
is driven to express himself in a seemingly confused or unintelligible way. In such cases only a careful inquiry into the why and
wherefore, and a conscientious deliberation of the answers, can
save the teacher from false judgments. But there are also cases
where the gift applies to some aptitude not affected by school-
work at all. This is particularly true of certain practical accom-
plishments. I myself remember boys who distinguished themselves at school by their remarkable stupidity, but who were
highly efficient at the peasant trades of their parents.

239   While I am on this subject I must not omit to point out that
very erroneous views used to be held at one time concerning the
gift for mathematics. It was believed that the capacity for logical
and abstract thought was, so to speak, incarnate in mathematics
and that this was therefore the best discipline if one wanted to
think logically. But the mathematical gift, like the musical gift
to which it is biologically related, is identical neither with logic
nor with intellect, although it makes use of them just as all
philosophy and science do. One can be musical without pos-
sessing a scrap of intellect, and in the same way astounding feats
of calculation can be performed by imbeciles. Mathematical
sense can be inculcated as little as can musical sense, for it is a
specific gift.

240   The gifted child is faced with complications not only in the
intellectual but in the moral sphere, that is, in the province of
feeling. The prevarication, lying, and other moral laxities so
common in grown-ups can easily become a distressing problem
for the morally gifted child. It is just as easy for an adult to disregard moral criticism that springs from feeling, as it is to overlook or underestimate intellectual sensitivity and precocity. The
gifts of the heart are not quite so obvious or so impressive as in-

139

tellectual and technical endowments, and, just as the latter demand special understanding from the teacher, so these other gifts often make the even greater demand that he himself should be educated. For the day will inevitably come when what the educator teaches by word of mouth no longer works, but only what he is. Every educator—and I use the term in its widest sense —should constantly ask himself whether he is actually fulfilling his teachings in his own person and in his own life, to the best of his knowledge and with a clear conscience. Psychotherapy has taught us that in the final reckoning it is not knowledge, not technical skill, that has a curative effect, but the personality of the doctor. And it is the same with education: it presupposes self-education.

241   In saying this I have no wish to set myself up as a judge over the pedagogues; on the contrary, with my many years as active teacher and educator, I must count myself as one of them and await judgment or condemnation with the rest. It is only on the basis of my experience in treating human beings that I venture to draw your attention to the profound practical significance of this fundamental educational truth.

242   There are, besides the gifts of the head, also those of the heart, which are no whit less important, although they may easily be overlooked because in such cases the head is often the weaker organ. And yet people of this kind sometimes contribute more to the well-being of society, and are more valuable, than those with other talents. But, like all gifts, talented feeling has two sides to it. A high degree of empathy, especially noticeable in girls, can adapt itself to the teacher so skilfully as to arouse the impression of a special talent, and moreover on the evidence of no mean achievements. But as soon as the personal influence ceases, the gift fizzles out. It was nothing but an enthusiastic episode conjured into existence through empathy, flaring up like a straw fire and leaving the ashes of disappointment behind.

243   The education of gifted children makes considerable demands upon the intellectual, psychological, moral, and artistic capacities of the educator, demands which, it may be, no teacher can reasonably be expected to fulfil. He would have to be something of a genius himself if he were to do justice to the gift of genius among any of his pupils.

244   Fortunately, however, many gifts seem to have a peculiar ability to take care of themselves, and the closer a gifted child comes to being a genius the more his creative capacity—as the very word "genius" implies—acts like a personality far in advance of his years, one might even say like a divine daemon who not only needs no educating, but against whom it is more necessary to protect the child. Great gifts are the fairest, and often the most dangerous, fruits on the tree of humanity. They hang on the weakest branches, which easily break. In most cases, as I have already suggested, the gift develops in inverse ratio to the maturation of the personality as a whole, and often one has the impression that a creative personality grows at the expense of the human being. Sometimes, indeed, there is such a discrepancy between the genius and his human qualities that one has to ask oneself whether a little less talent might not have been better. What after all is great intellect beside moral inferiority? There are not a few gifted persons whose usefulness is paralysed, not to say perverted, by their human shortcomings. A gift is not an absolute value, or rather, it is such a value only when the rest of the personality keeps pace with it, so that the talent can be applied usefully. Creative powers can just as easily turn out to be destructive. It rests solely with the moral personality whether they apply themselves to good things or to bad. And if this is lacking, no teacher can supply it or take its place.

245   The narrow margin between a gift and its pathological variant makes the problem of educating such children much more difficult. Not only is the gift almost invariably compensated by some inferiority in another sphere, but occasionally it is coupled with a morbid defect. In such cases it is almost impossible to determine whether it is the gift or the psychopathic constitution that predominates.

246   For all these reasons I would hardly like to say whether it would be of advantage to educate particularly gifted pupils in separate classes, as has been proposed.[2] I at least would not care to be the expert upon whom devolved the selection of suitable pupils. Although it would be an enormous help to the gifted ones, we have still to consider the fact that these same pupils do

2 [By and large, children in Switzerland are taught in classes composed of pupils belonging to the same age group. There is no attempt to separate them according to their ability as is usual in Great Britain.—EDITORS.]

not always come up to the level of their gifts in other respects, human as well as mental. Segregated in a special class, the gifted child would be in danger of developing into a one-sided product. In a normal class, on the other hand, although he might be bored with the subject in which he excelled, the other subjects would serve to remind him of his backwardness, and this would have a useful and much-needed moral effect. For all gifts have the moral disadvantage of causing in their possessor a feeling of superiority and hence an inflation which needs to be compensated by a corresponding humility. But since gifted children are very often spoilt, they come to expect exceptional treatment. My old teacher was well aware of this, and that is why he delivered his moral "knock-out," from which I failed at the time to draw the necessary conclusions. Since then I have learnt to see that my teacher was an instrument of fate. He was the first to give me a taste of the hard truth that the gifts of the gods have two sides, a bright and a dark. To rush ahead is to invite blows, and if you don't get them from the teacher, you will get them from fate, and generally from both. The gifted child will do well to accustom himself early to the fact that any excellence puts him in an exceptional position and exposes him to a great many risks, the chief of which is an exaggerated self-confidence. Against this the only protection is humility and obedience, and even these do not always work.

247   It therefore seems to me better to educate the gifted child along with the other children in a normal class, and not to underline his exceptional position by transferring him to a special class. When all is said and done, school is a part of the great world and contains in miniature all those factors which the child will encounter in later life and with which he will have to come to terms. Some at least of this necessary adaptation can and should be learnt at school. Occasional clashes are not a catastrophe. Misunderstanding is fatal only when chronic, or when the child's sensitivity is unusually acute and there is no possibility of finding another teacher. That often brings favourable results, but only when the cause of the trouble really does lie with the teacher. This is by no means the rule, for in many cases the teacher has to suffer for the ruin wrought by the child's upbringing at home. Far too often parents who were unable to fulfil their own ambitions embody them in their gifted child,

whom they either pamper or else whip up into a showpiece, sometimes very much to his detriment in later years, as is sufficiently evident from the lives of certain infant prodigies.

248   A powerful talent, and especially the Danaän gift of genius, is a fateful factor that throws its shadow early before. The genius will come through despite everything, for there is something absolute and indomitable in ʌis nature. The so-called "misunderstood genius" is rather a doubtful phenomenon. Generally he turns out to be a good-for-nothing who is forever seeking a soothing explanation of himself. Once, in my professional capacity, I was forced to confront a "genius" of this type with the alternative: "Or perhaps you are nothing but a lazy hound?" It was not long before we found ourselves in whole-hearted agreement on this point. Talent, on the other hand, can either be hampered, crippled, and perverted, or fostered, developed, and improved. The genius is as rare a bird as the phoenix, an apparition not to be counted upon. Consciously or unconsciously, genius is something that by God's grace is there from the start, in full strength. But talent is a statistical regularity and does not always have a dynamism to match. Like genius, it is exceedingly diverse in its forms, giving rise to individual differentiations which the educator ought not to overlook; for a differentiated personality, or one capable of differentiation, is of the utmost value to the community. The levelling down of the masses through suppression of the aristocratic or hierarchical structure natural to a community is bound, sooner or later, to lead to disaster. For, when everything outstanding is levelled down, the signposts are lost, and the longing to be led becomes an urgent necessity. Human leadership being fallible, the leader himself has always been, and always will be, subject to the great symbolical principles, even as the individual cannot give his life point and meaning unless he puts his ego at the service of a spiritual authority superordinate to man. The need to do this arises from the fact that the ego never constitutes the whole of a man, but only the conscious part of him. The unconscious part, of unlimited extent, alone can complete him and make him a real totality.

249   Biologically speaking, the gifted person is a deviation from the mean, and in so far as Lao-tzu's remark that "high stands on low" is one of the eternal verities, this deviation takes place si-

multaneously in the heights and depths of the same individual. This produces a tension of opposites in him, which in its turn tempers and intensifies his personality. Like the still waters, the gifted child runs deep. His danger lies not only in deviating from the norm, however favourable this may appear to be, but even more in that inner polarity which predisposes to conflict. Therefore, instead of segregation in special classes, the personal interest and attention of the teacher are likely to be more beneficial. Although the institution of a trained school psychiatrist is thoroughly to be recommended and need not be a mere concession to the craze for what is technically right, I would say, in the light of my own experience, that an understanding heart is everything in a teacher, and cannot be esteemed highly enough. One looks back with appreciation to the brilliant teachers, but with gratitude to those who touched our human feelings. The curriculum is so much necessary raw material, but warmth is the vital element for the growing plant and for the soul of the child.

250   Because there are, among the other pupils, gifted and highly strung natures which ought not to be hemmed in and stifled, the school curriculum should for that very reason never wander too far from the humanities into over-specialized fields. The coming generation should at least be shown the doors that lead to the many different departments of life and the mind. And it seems to me especially important for any broad-based culture to have a regard for history in the widest sense of the word. Important as it is to pay attention to what is practical and useful, and to consider the future, that backward glance at the past is just as important. Culture means continuity, not a tearing up of roots through "progress." For the gifted child in particular, a balanced education is essential as a measure of psychic hygiene. As I have said, his gift is one-sided and is almost always offset by some childish immaturity in other regions of the psyche. Childhood, however, is a state of the past. Just as the developing embryo recapitulates, in a sense, our phylogenetic history, so the child-psyche relives "the lesson of earlier humanity," as Nietzsche called it. The child lives in a pre-rational and above all in a pre-scientific world, the world of the men who existed before us. Our roots lie in that world and every child grows from those roots. Maturity bears him away from his roots and immaturity binds him to them. Knowledge of the universal origins builds

the bridge between the lost and abandoned world of the past and the still largely inconceivable world of the future. How should we lay hold of the future, how should we assimilate it, unless we are in possession of the human experience which the past has bequeathed to us? Dispossessed of this, we are without root and without perspective, defenceless dupes of whatever novelties the future may bring. A purely technical and practical education is no safeguard against delusion and has nothing to oppose to the counterfeit. It lacks the culture whose innermost law is the continuity of history, the long procession of man's more than individual consciousness. This continuity which reconciles all opposites also heals the conflicts that threaten the gifted child.

251   Anything new should always be questioned and tested with caution, for it may very easily turn out to be only a new disease. That is why true progress is impossible without mature judgment. But a well-balanced judgment requires a firm standpoint, and this in turn can only rest on a sound knowledge of what has been. The man who is unconscious of the historical context and lets slip his link with the past is in constant danger of succumbing to the crazes and delusions engendered by all novelties. It is the tragedy of all innovators that they empty out the baby with the bath-water. Though the mania for novelty is not, thank heavens, the national vice of the Swiss, we live nevertheless in a wider world that is being shaken by strange fevers of renewal. In face of this frightening and grandiose spectacle, steadiness is demanded of our young men as never before, firstly for the stability of our country, and secondly for the sake of European civilization, which has nothing to gain if the achievements of the Christian past are wiped out.

252   The gifted ones, however, are the torch-bearers, chosen for that high office by nature herself.

VI

THE SIGNIFICANCE OF THE
UNCONSCIOUS
IN INDIVIDUAL EDUCATION

THE SIGNIFICANCE OF THE UNCONSCIOUS
IN INDIVIDUAL EDUCATION [1]

253   In general, one can distinguish three kinds of education:
I. EDUCATION THROUGH EXAMPLE. This kind of education can
proceed wholly unconsciously and is therefore the oldest and
perhaps the most effective form of all. It is aided by the fact that
the child is psychologically more or less identical with its environment, and especially with its parents. This peculiarity is one
of the most conspicuous features of the primitive psyche, for
which the French anthropologist, Lévy-Bruhl, coined the term
"participation mystique." Because unconscious education
through example rests on one of the oldest psychic characteristics, it is effective where all other direct methods fail, as for
instance in insanity. Many insane patients have to be made to
work in order to keep them from degenerating: to give them
advice, or to try to order them about, is in most cases quite useless. But if you just send them along with a group of workers,
eventually they get infected by the example of the others and
begin to work themselves. In the last analysis, all education rests
on this fundamental fact of psychic identity, and in all cases the

1 [Originally delivered as a lecture at the International Congress of Education,
Heidelberg, 1925, and subsequently translated by C. F. and H. G. Baynes in
Contributions to Analytical Psychology (London and New York, 1928). The pres-
ent translation is newly made from the original manuscript, though the earlier
English version has been freely consulted.—EDITORS.]

deciding factor is this seemingly automatic contagion through example. This is so important that even the best methods of conscious education can sometimes be completely nullified by bad example.

254   II. COLLECTIVE EDUCATION. By collective education I do not necessarily mean education *en masse* (as in schools), but education according to rules, principles, and methods. These three things are necessarily of a collective nature, since it is assumed that they are at least valid for and applicable to the large majority of individuals. It is further assumed that they are effective instruments in the hands of all those who have learnt how to manipulate them. We can take it for granted that this kind of education will not produce anything except what is already contained in its premises, and that the individuals it turns out will be moulded by general rules, principles, and methods.

255   To the extent that the individuality of the pupil succumbs to the collective nature of these educational influences, he naturally develops a character much resembling that of another individual, who, though originally quite different, has nevertheless acquiesced in the same way. If there is a large number of individuals who possess this degree of acquiescence, conformity becomes uniformity. The larger the number of individuals who conform, the greater the unconscious pressure of example on all those who, rightly or wrongly, have so far successfully resisted the collective method. And since the example of the crowd exerts a compelling influence through unconscious psychic contagion, it may in the long run have a crushing effect upon those individuals who possess no more than average strength of character, if it does not extinguish them altogether. Provided that the quality of this training is sound, we may naturally expect good results so far as collective adaptation is concerned. On the other hand, an over-idealistic moulding of character can have disastrous consequences for the unique personality of the individual. To educate him into being a good citizen and a useful member of society is certainly a highly desirable goal. But once a certain level of uniformity is overstepped, and collective values are fostered at the expense of individual uniqueness, then you get the type of person who, though he may be a perfect paragon of the educational rules, principles, and methods, and is therefore adapted to all the situations and problems that come within

the scope of his educational premises, nevertheless feels insecure in all matters where individual judgments have to be made without recourse to the regulations.

256   Collective education is indeed a necessity and cannot be replaced by anything else. We live in a collective world, and we need collective norms just as much as we need a common language. On no account must the principle of collective education be sacrificed for the sake of developing individual idiosyncrasies, however much we may desire to prevent the more valuable ones from being stifled. We must bear in mind that individual uniqueness is not under all circumstances an asset, not even for the individual himself. When we examine the type of child who resists collective education, we often find that these children are afflicted with various psychic abnormalities, either congenital or acquired. Among them I would also include spoiled and demoralized children. Many such children actually work out their own salvation by throwing themselves on the support of a normally functioning group. In this way they achieve a certain degree of uniformity, and can protect themselves from the injurious effects of their own individualities. I do not at all subscribe to the view that fundamentally man is always good, and that his evil qualities are merely misunderstood good. On the contrary, I hold that there are very many persons who represent such an inferior combination of inherited characteristics that it would be far better both for society and for themselves if they refrained from expressing their individual idiosyncrasies. We can therefore claim with a clear conscience that collective education is, at bottom, of undoubted value, and absolutely sufficient for most people. We must not, however, make it the sovereign principle of education, for there exists a large group of children who require the third form of education, namely *individual* education.

257   III. INDIVIDUAL EDUCATION. In applying this method, all rules, principles, and systems must be subordinated to the one purpose of bringing out the specific individuality of the pupil. This aim is directly opposed to that of collective education, which seeks to level out and make uniform. All children who successfully resist this require individual attention. Among these we naturally find the most diverse types. First of all, there are those who are ineducable as a result of pathological degeneration. These generally fall into the category of mental defectives. Then

there are others who, far from being ineducable, exhibit special aptitudes, though of a peculiar or one-sided nature. The most frequent of such peculiarities is the incapacity to understand any form of mathematics not expressed in concrete numbers. For this reason higher mathematics ought always to be optional in schools, since it is in no way connected with the development of logical thinking. For these pupils, mathematics is quite meaningless, and a source of needless torment. The truth is that mathematics presupposes a definite mental aptitude which by no means everybody possesses and which cannot be acquired. For those who do not possess it, mathematics can only be learnt by rote like a jumble of meaningless words. Such persons may be highly gifted in every other way, and may possess the capacity for logical thinking already, or can acquire it more easily through direct instruction in logic.

258   Strictly speaking, of course, a deficiency in mathematical ability cannot be regarded as an individual peculiarity. But it does clearly show how a school curriculum may sin against the psychological peculiarity of a pupil. In the same way, certain widely accepted pedagogic principles may prove to be utterly useless, indeed positively harmful, in all cases where the psychological peculiarity of the pupil calls for an exclusively individual influence. Fairly frequently we find that not only specific rules, but the whole apparatus of educational influence is met by an insurmountable antagonism. In such cases we usually have to do with so-called neurotic children. The teacher is at first inclined to ascribe the difficulties to the morbid disposition of the child, but more careful inquiry will often show that the child comes from a peculiar domestic milieu which is quite sufficient to explain his maladjustment. The child has acquired an attitude at home that unfits him for collective life.

259   It is, of course, quite outside the teacher's province to change the home atmosphere, although a little good advice can often work wonders even with parents. As a rule, however, the trouble has to be cured in the child himself, and this means finding the right approach to his peculiar psychology so as to render it amenable to influence. As we have already said, the first requisite is thorough knowledge of his home life. We know a great deal when we have found out the causes of a symptom, but still more is needed. The next thing we need to know is what sort of effects

the external causes have produced in the child's psyche. This knowledge we obtain from a thorough investigation of his psychological life-history on the basis of his own and his parents' statements. Under certain conditions a good deal can be accomplished with just this information. Skilful teachers have applied this method all along, so there is no need for me to dwell on it here.

260   If we realize that the child gradually develops out of the unconscious state into a conscious one, we can understand why practically all environmental influences, or at any rate the most elementary and most lasting of them, are unconscious. The first impressions of life are the strongest and most profound, even though they are unconscious—perhaps indeed for that very reason, for so long as they are unconscious they are not subject to change. We can only correct what is in our consciousness; what is unconscious remains unchanged. Consequently, if we wish to produce a change we must first raise these unconscious contents to consciousness, so as to submit them to correction. This operation is not necessary in cases where a careful investigation of the family environment and of the psychological life-history of the individual has furnished us with the means of influencing him effectively. But in cases where this does not suffice, the investigation must go deeper. It is a species of surgical intervention which can have dire results if performed without adequate technical equipment. It takes considerable medical experience to know just when and where this treatment should be applied. Laymen unfortunately often underestimate the dangers which such interventions entail. By bringing unconscious contents to the surface you artificially create a condition that bears the closest resemblance to a psychosis. The vast majority of mental illnesses (except those of a directly organic nature) are due to a disintegration of consciousness caused by the irresistible invasion of unconscious contents. Accordingly we must know where we can intervene without the risk of harm. Even if no danger threatens from this side, we are still not exempt from certain hazards. One of the commonest consequences of preoccupation with unconscious contents is the development of what Freud called "the transference." Strictly speaking, transference is the projection of unconscious contents upon the person analysing the unconscious. The term "transference," however, is used in

a much wider sense and embraces all the exceedingly complex processes which bind the patient to the analyst. This bond can turn into an extremely unpleasant obstacle if inexpertly handled. There are cases where it has even led to suicide. One of the main reasons for this is the coming to consciousness of certain unconscious contents which throw a new and disturbing light on the family situation. Things may come up that transform the patient's love and trust in his parents into resistance and hatred. He then finds himself in an intolerable state of isolation, and will cling desperately to the analyst as his last remaining link with the world. If at this critical juncture the analyst, through some technical blunder, snaps even this link, it can lead straight to suicide.

261   I am therefore of the opinion that so drastic a measure as the analysis of the unconscious should at least be conducted under the control and guidance of a doctor adequately trained in psychiatry and psychology.

262   In what way, then, can unconscious contents be brought to consciousness? As you will realize, it is hardly possible within the compass of a lecture to describe all the ways in which this may be done. The best practical method, though also the most difficult, is the analysis and interpretation of dreams. Dreams are unquestionably products of unconscious psychic activity. Born in sleep without design or assistance on our part, they pass before our inward vision and may suddenly float back into our waking life on a dim remnant of consciousness. Their strange, often irrational and incomprehensible nature may well inspire mistrust of them as reliable sources of information. And indeed our attempts to understand dreams are scarcely in keeping with any known scientific method of calculation and measurement. Our position is more like that of an archaeologist deciphering an unknown script. Yet, if unconscious contents exist at all, dreams are surely in the best position to tell us something about them. To Freud belongs the great honour of having been the first to demonstrate this possibility in our own day, although all previous ages were deeply preoccupied with the mystery of dreams, nor was this interest always purely superstitious. The work of Artemidorus of Daldis (second century A.D.) on dream interpretation is, of its kind, a scientific document not to be despised, nor should we dismiss as valueless the dream interpre-

tations of the Essenes recorded by Flavius Josephus (b. A.D. 37). Nevertheless, had it not been for Freud, science would probably not have returned so soon to dreams as sources of information, despite the enormous attention paid to them by the physicians of antiquity. Even today opinion is still very much divided on this subject. There are in fact many medical psychologists who refuse to analyse dreams, either because the method seems to them too uncertain, too arbitrary, and too difficult, or because they feel no need of the unconscious. I myself am of the contrary opinion, and have been convinced by ample experience that in all difficult cases the patient's dreams can be of incalculable value to the psychiatrist, both as a source of information and as a therapeutic instrument.

263   Coming now to the much-disputed question of dream-analysis, we proceed in a manner not unlike that employed in the deciphering of hieroglyphs. First we assemble all the available material which the dreamer himself can give as regards the dream images. We next exclude any statements that depend upon particular theoretical assumptions, for those are generally quite arbitrary attempts at interpretation. We then inquire into the happenings of the previous day, as well as into the mood and the general plans and purposes of the dreamer in the days and weeks preceding the dream. A more or less intimate knowledge of his circumstances and character is of course a necessary prerequisite. Great care and attention must be given to this preparatory work if we want to get at the meaning of the dream. I have no faith in dream interpretations made on the spur of the moment and concocted out of some preconceived theory. One must be careful not to impose any theoretical assumptions on the dream; in fact, it is always best to proceed as if the dream had no meaning at all, so as to be on one's guard against any possible bias. Dream-analysis may yield entirely unforeseen results, and facts of an exceedingly disagreeable nature may sometimes come to light whose discussion would certainly have been avoided at all costs had we been able to anticipate them. We may also get results that are obscure and unintelligible at first, because our conscious standpoint has still not plumbed the secrets of the psyche. In such cases it is better to adopt a waiting attitude than to attempt a forced explanation. In this kind of work one has to put up with a great many question marks.

264   While we are engaged in collecting all this material certain portions of the dream gradually grow clearer, and we begin to see, in the apparently meaningless jumble of images, some glimmerings of a script—only disconnected sentences at first, then more and more of the context. It will perhaps be best if I give you a few examples of the dreams that occur in the course of an individual education under medical control.[2]

265   I must first acquaint you in some measure with the personality of the dreamer, for without this acquaintance you will hardly be able to transport yourselves into the peculiar atmosphere of the dreams.

266   There are dreams that are pure poems and can therefore only be understood through the mood they convey as a whole. The dreamer is a youth of a little over twenty, still entirely boyish in appearance. There is even a touch of girlishness in his looks and manner of expression. The latter betrays a very good education and upbringing. He is intelligent, with pronounced intellectual and aesthetic interests. His aestheticism is very much in evidence: we are made instantly aware of his good taste and his fine appreciation of all forms of art. His feelings are tender and soft, given to the enthusiasms typical of puberty, but somewhat effeminate. There is no trace of adolescent callowness. Undoubtedly he is too young for his age, a clear case of retarded development. It is quite in keeping with this that he should have come to me on account of his homosexuality. The night preceding his first visit he had the following dream:

"I am in a lofty cathedral filled with mysterious twilight. They tell me that it is the cathedral at Lourdes. In the centre there is a deep dark well, into which I have to descend."

267   The dream is clearly a coherent expression of mood. The dreamer's comments are as follows: "Lourdes is the mystic fount of healing. Naturally I remembered yesterday that I was going to you for treatment and was in search of a cure. There is said to be a well like this at Lourdes. It would be rather unpleasant to go down into the water. The well was ever so deep."

268   Now what does this dream tell us? On the surface it seems clear enough, and we might be content to take it as a kind of poetic formulation of the mood of the day before. But we should

2 [This case is also discussed in *Two Essays on Analytical Psychology, Coll. Works*, Vol. 7, pars. 167ff.—EDITORS.]

never stop there, for experience shows that dreams are much deeper and more significant. One might almost suppose that the dreamer came to the doctor in a highly poetic mood and was entering upon the treatment as though it were a sacred religious act to be performed in the mystical half-light of some awe-inspiring sanctuary. But this does not fit the facts at all. The patient merely came to the doctor to be treated for that unpleasant matter, his homosexuality, which is anything but poetic. At any rate we cannot see from the mood of the preceding day why he should dream so poetically, if we were to accept so direct a causation for the origin of the dream. But we might conjecture, perhaps, that the dream was stimulated precisely by the dreamer's impressions of that highly unpoetical affair which impelled him to come to me for treatment. We might even suppose that he dreamed in such an intensely poetical manner just because of the unpoeticalness of his mood on the day before, much as a man who has fasted by day dreams of delicious meals at night. It cannot be denied that the thought of treatment, of the cure and its unpleasant procedure, recurs in the dream, but poetically transfigured, and in a guise which meets most effectively the lively aesthetic and emotional needs of the dreamer. He will be drawn on irresistibly by this inviting picture, despite the fact that the well is dark, deep, and cold. Something of the dream-mood will persist after sleep and will even linger on into the morning of the day on which he has to submit to the unpleasant and unpoetical duty of visiting me. Perhaps the drab reality will be touched by the bright, golden after-glow of the dream feeling.

269   Is this, perhaps, the purpose of the dream? That would not be impossible, for in my experience the vast majority of dreams are compensatory. They always stress the other side in order to maintain the psychic equilibrium. But the compensation of mood is not the only purpose of the dream picture. The dream also provides a mental corrective. The patient had of course nothing like an adequate understanding of the treatment to which he was about to submit himself. But the dream gives him a picture which describes in poetic metaphors the nature of the treatment before him. This becomes immediately apparent if we follow up his associations and comments on the image of the cathedral:

"Cathedral," he says, "makes me think of Cologne Cathedral.

157

Even as a child I was fascinated by it. I remember my mother telling me of it for the first time, and I also remember how, whenever I saw a village church, I asked if it were Cologne Cathedral. I wanted to be a priest in a cathedral like that."

270   In these associations the patient is describing a very important experience of his childhood. As in nearly all cases of this kind, he had a particularly close tie with his mother. By this we are not to understand a particularly good or intense *conscious* relationship, but something in the nature of a secret, subterranean tie which expresses itself consciously, perhaps, only in the retarded development of character, i.e., in a relative infantilism. The developing personality naturally veers away from such an unconscious infantile bond; for nothing is more obstructive to development than persistence in an unconscious—one could also say, a psychically embryonic, condition. For this reason instinct seizes on the first opportunity to replace the mother by another object. If it is to be a real mother-substitute, this object must be, in some sense, an analogy of her. This is entirely the case with our patient. The intensity with which his childish fantasy seized upon the symbol of Cologne Cathedral corresponds to the strength of his unconscious need to find a substitute for the mother. The unconscious need is heightened still further in a case where the infantile bond threatens injury. Hence the enthusiasm with which his childish imagination took up the idea of the Church; for the Church is, in the fullest sense, a mother. We speak not only of Mother Church, but even of the Church's womb. In the ceremony known as the *benedictio fontis,* the baptismal font is apostrophized as *immaculatus divini fontis uterus*—"immaculate womb of the divine fount." We naturally think that a man must have known this meaning consciously before it could get to work on his fantasy, and that an unknowing child could not possibly be affected by these significations. Such analogies certainly do not work by way of the conscious mind, but in quite another manner.

271   The Church represents a higher spiritual substitute for the purely natural, or "carnal," tie to the parents. Consequently it frees the individual from an unconscious natural relationship which, strictly speaking, is not a relationship at all but simply a condition of inchoate, unconscious identity. This, just because it is unconscious, possesses a tremendous inertia and offers the ut-

most resistance to any kind of spiritual development. It would be hard to say what the essential difference is between this condition and the soul of an animal. Now, it is by no means the special prerogative of the Christian Church to try to make it possible for the individual to detach himself from his original, animal-like condition; the Church is simply the latest, and specifically Western, form of an instinctive striving that is probably as old as mankind itself. It is a striving that can be found in the most varied forms among all primitive peoples who are in any way developed and have not yet become degenerate: I mean the institution or rite of initiation into manhood. When he has reached puberty the young man is conducted to the "men's house," or some other place of consecration, where he is systematically alienated from his family. At the same time he is initiated into the religious mysteries, and in this way is ushered not only into a wholly new set of relationships, but, as a renewed and changed personality, into a new world, like one reborn (*quasi modo genitus*). The initiation is often attended by all kinds of tortures, sometimes including circumcision and the like. These practices are undoubtedly very old. They have almost become instinctive mechanisms, with the result that they continue to repeat themselves without external compulsion, as in the "baptisms" of German students or the even more wildly extravagant initiations in American students' fraternities. They have become engraved in the unconscious in the form of a primordial image, an archetype, as St. Augustine calls it.

272   When his mother told him as a little boy about Cologne Cathedral, this primordial image was stirred and awakened to life. But there was no priestly instructor to develop it further, so the child remained in his mother's hands. Yet the longing for a man's leadership continued to grow in the boy, taking the form of homosexual leanings—a faulty development that might never have come about had a man been there to educate his childish fantasies. The deviation towards homosexuality has, to be sure, numerous historical precedents. In ancient Greece, as also in certain primitive communities, homosexuality and education were practically synonymous. Viewed in this light, the homosexuality of adolescence is only a profound misunderstanding of the otherwise very appropriate need for masculine guidance.

273   According to the dream, then, what the initiation of the treatment signifies for the patient is the fulfilment of the true meaning of his homosexuality, i.e., his entry into the world of adult men. All that we have been forced to discuss here in such tedious and long-winded detail, in order to understand it properly, the dream has condensed into a few vivid metaphors, thus creating a picture which works far more effectively on the imagination, feeling, and understanding of the dreamer than any learned discourse. Consequently the patient was better and more intelligently prepared for the treatment than if he had been overwhelmed with medical and pedagogical maxims. For this reason I regard dreams not only as a valuable source of information but as an extraordinarily effective instrument of education and therapy.

274   I shall now give you the second dream, which the patient dreamt on the night following his first visit to me. It makes certain welcome additions to the previous one. I must explain in advance that during the first consultation I did not refer in any way to the dream we have just been discussing. It was not even mentioned. Nor was there a word said that was even remotely connected with the foregoing.

275   The second dream was as follows:

"I am in a great Gothic cathedral. At the altar stands a priest. I stand before him with my friend, holding in my hand a little Japanese ivory figure, with the feeling that it is going to be baptized. Suddenly an elderly woman appears, takes the fraternity ring from my friend's finger, and puts it on her own. My friend is afraid that this may bind him in some way. But at the same time there is a sound of wonderful organ music."

276   Unfortunately I cannot, within the short space of a lecture, enter into all the details of this exceedingly ingenious dream. Here I will only bring out briefly those points which continue and supplement the dream of the preceding day. The second dream is unmistakably connected with the first: once more the dreamer is in church, that is, in the state of initiation into manhood. But a new figure has been added: the priest, whose absence in the previous situation we have already noted. The dream therefore confirms that the unconscious meaning of his homosexuality has been fulfilled and that a new development can be started. The actual initiation ceremony, that is, the bap-

tism, may now begin. The dream symbolism corroborates what I said before, namely that it is not the prerogative of the Christian Church to bring about such transitions and psychic transformations, but that behind the Church there is a living primordial image which in certain conditions is capable of enforcing them.

277   What, according to the dream, is to be baptized is a little Japanese ivory figure. The patient says of this: "It was a tiny, grotesque little manikin that reminded me of the male organ. It was certainly odd that this member was to be baptized. But after all, with the Jews circumcision is a sort of baptism. That must be a reference to my homosexuality, because the friend standing with me before the altar is the one with whom I have sexual relations. We belong to the same fraternity. The fraternity ring obviously stands for our relationship."

278   We know that in common usage the ring is the token of a bond or relationship, as for example the wedding ring. We can therefore safely take the fraternity ring in this case as symbolizing the homosexual relationship, and the fact that the dreamer appears together with his friend points in the same direction.

279   The complaint to be remedied is homosexuality. The dreamer is to be led out of this relatively childish condition and initiated into the adult state by means of a kind of circumcision ceremony under the supervision of a priest. These ideas correspond exactly to my analysis of the previous dream. Thus far the development has proceeded logically and consistently with the aid of archetypal images. But now a disturbing factor appears to enter. An elderly woman suddenly takes possession of the fraternity ring; in other words, she draws to herself what has hitherto been a homosexual relationship, thus causing the dreamer to fear that he is getting involved in a new relationship with obligations of its own. Since the ring is now on the hand of a woman, a marriage of sorts has been contracted, i.e., the homosexual relationship seems to have passed over into a heterosexual one, but a heterosexual relationship of a peculiar kind, as it concerns an elderly woman. "She is a friend of my mother's," says the patient. "I am very fond of her, in fact she is like a mother to me." From this remark we can see what has happened in the dream: as a result of the initiation the homosexual tie has been cut and a heterosexual relationship substituted for it, a platonic friendship with a woman resembling his mother. In spite of her resem-

161

blance to his mother, this woman is not his mother any longer, so the relationship with her signifies a step beyond the mother towards masculinity, and hence a partial conquest of his adolescent homosexuality.

280   The fear of the new tie can easily be understood, firstly as the fear which the woman's resemblance to his mother might naturally arouse—it could be argued that the dissolution of the homosexual tie has led to a complete regression to the mother— and secondly as the fear of the new and unknown factors in the adult heterosexual state with its possible obligations, such as marriage, and so on. That we are in fact concerned here not with a regression but with an advance seems to be confirmed by the music that now peals forth. The patient is musical and especially susceptible to solemn organ music. Therefore music signifies for him a very positive feeling, so in this case it forms an harmonious conclusion to the dream, which in turn is well qualified to leave behind a beautiful, holy feeling for the following morning.

281   If you consider the fact that up to now the patient had seen me for only one consultation, in which little more was discussed than a general anamnesis, you will doubtless agree with me when I say that both dreams make astonishing anticipations. They show the patient's situation in a highly remarkable light, and one that is very strange to the conscious mind, while at the same time they lend to the banal medical situation an aspect that is uniquely attuned to the psychic peculiarities of the dreamer, and thus capable of stringing his aesthetic, intellectual, and religious interests to concert pitch. No better conditions for treatment could possibly be imagined. One is almost persuaded, from the meaning of these dreams, that the patient entered upon the treatment with the utmost readiness and hopefulness, quite prepared to cast aside his boyishness and become a man. In reality, however, this was not the case at all. Consciously he was full of hesitation and resistance; moreover, as the treatment progressed, he constantly showed himself antagonistic and difficult, ever ready to slip back into his previous infantilism. The dreams, therefore, stand in strict contrast to his conscious behaviour. They move along a progressive line and are on the side of the educator. In my opinion they give us a clear view of the specific function of dreams. This function I have called compensation.

The unconscious progressiveness and the conscious regressiveness together form a pair of opposites which, as it were, keeps the scales balanced. The influence of the educator tilts the balance in favour of progression. In this way dreams give effective support to our educational efforts and at the same time afford the deepest insight into the intimate fantasy life of the patient. Thus his conscious attitude gradually becomes more understanding and receptive to new influences.

282 From what has been said it might be inferred that, were all dreams to behave in this manner, they would be an incomparable means of access to the most individual secrets of psychic life. In so far as dreams are capable of explanation, this is actually true as a general rule; but the great difficulty nevertheless remains of explaining them. Not only is wide experience and considerable tact needed, but also knowledge. To interpret dreams on the basis of a general theory, or on certain ready-made suppositions, is not merely ineffectual, but a definitely wrong and harmful practice. By the gentle art of persuasion and by the liberal use of alleged dream-mechanisms like inversion, distortion, displacement and what not, the dream can be construed to yield almost any meaning. The same arbitrary procedures were also to be found in the first attempts to decipher hieroglyphs. Before even attempting to understand a dream we ought always to say to ourselves, "This dream can mean anything." It need not stand in opposition to the conscious attitude, but may simply run parallel to it, which would also be quite in accord with its compensatory function. Moreover, there are dreams that defy every effort at interpretation. Often the only possible thing is to hazard a guess. At any rate, up to the present no open sesame for dreams has been discovered, no infallible method, and no absolutely satisfactory theory. The Freudian hypothesis that all dreams are the disguised fulfilment of sexual and other morally inadmissible wishes I myself cannot corroborate. I must therefore regard the use of this hypothesis and the tactics based upon it as a subjective bias. Indeed, I am persuaded that, in view of the tremendous irrationality and individuality of dreams, it may be altogether outside the bounds of possibility to construct a popular theory. Why should we believe that everything without exception is a fit subject for science? Scientific thinking is only one of the mental faculties at our

disposal for understanding the world. It might be better to look upon dreams as being more in the nature of works of art instead of mere observational data for the scientist. The first view seems to me to yield better results because it is nearer to the essential nature of dreams. And this, after all, is the main point, that we should make ourselves aware of our unconscious compensation and thus overcome the one-sidedness and inadequacy of the conscious attitude. So long as other methods of education are efficacious and useful, we do not need the assistance of the unconscious. Indeed it would be a most reprehensible blunder if we tried to substitute analysis of the unconscious for well-tried conscious methods. The analytical method should be strictly reserved for those cases where other methods have failed, and should then be practised only by specialists, or by laymen under specialist control and guidance.

283   The general results of such psychiatric studies and methods are not of mere academic interest to the educator; they may also be of very real help, since in certain cases they furnish him with an insight unattainable without such knowledge.

VII

THE DEVELOPMENT OF PERSONALITY

THE DEVELOPMENT OF PERSONALITY [1]

284   In somewhat free-handed fashion the last two lines of Goethe's stanza are often quoted:

> The Highest bliss on earth shall be
> The joys of personality! [2]

This gives expression to the view that the ultimate aim and strongest desire of all mankind is to develop that fulness of life which is called personality. Nowadays, "personality training" has become an educational ideal that turns its back upon the standardized, mass-produced, "normal" human being demanded by the machine age. It thus pays tribute to the historical fact that the great liberating deeds of world history have sprung from leading personalities and never from the inert mass, which is at all times secondary and can only be prodded into activity by the demagogue. The huzzahs of the Italian nation go forth to the personality of the Duce, and the dirges of other nations

---

[1] [First delivered as a lecture entitled "Die Stimme des Innern" at the Kulturbund, Vienna, in November, 1932. Subsequently published under the title "Vom Werden der Persönlichkeit" in *Wirklichkeit der Seele* (Zurich, Leipzig, and Stuttgart, 1934), and translated into English by Stanley M. Dell as the final chapter of *The Integration of the Personality* (New York, 1939, and London, 1940). The present new translation is made from *Wirklichkeit der Seele*, though the earlier English version has been freely consulted.—EDITORS.]

[2] *Westöstlicher Diwan*, Suleikabuch.

lament the absence of strong leaders.[3] The yearning for personality has therefore become a real problem that occupies many minds today, whereas in former times there was only one man who had a glimmering of this question—Friedrich Schiller, whose letters on aesthetic education have lain dormant, like a Sleeping Beauty of literature, for more than a century. We may confidently assert that the "Holy Roman Empire of the German Nation" has not taken much notice of Schiller as an educator. On the other hand, the *furor teutonicus* has hurled itself upon pedagogics (in the strict sense of the education of children), delved into child psychology, ferreted out the infantilism of the adult, and made of childhood such a portentous condition of life and human fate that it completely overshadows the creative meaning and potentialities of adult existence. Our age has been extravagantly praised as the "century of the child." This boundless expansion of the kindergarten amounts to complete forgetfulness of the problems of adult education divined by the genius of Schiller. Nobody will deny or underestimate the importance of childhood; the severe and often life-long injuries caused by stupid upbringing at home or in school are too obvious, and the need for more reasonable pedagogic methods is far too urgent. But if this evil is to be attacked at the root, one must in all seriousness face the question of how such idiotic and bigoted methods of education ever came to be employed, and still are employed. Obviously, for the sole reason that there are half-baked educators who are not human beings at all, but walking personifications of method. Anyone who wants to educate must himself be educated. But the parrot-like book-learning and mechanical use of methods that is still practised today is no education either for the child or for educator. People are everlastingly saying that the child's personality must be trained. While I admire this lofty ideal, I can't help asking who it is that trains the personality? In the first and foremost place we have the parents, ordinary, incompetent folk who, more often than not, are half children themselves and remain so all their lives. How could anyone expect all these ordinary parents to be "personalities," and who has ever given a thought to devising methods for inculcating "personality" into them? Naturally, then, we expect great things of the pedagogue, of the trained pro-

[3] After this was written, Germany also turned to a Führer.

168

fessional, who, heaven help us, has been stuffed full of "psychology" and is bursting with ill-assorted views as to how the child is supposed to be constituted and how he ought to be handled. It is presumed that the youthful persons who have picked on education as a career are themselves educated; but nobody, I daresay, will venture to assert that they are all "personalities" as well. By and large, they suffer from the same defective education as the hapless children they are supposed to instruct, and as a rule are as little "personalities" as their charges. Our whole educational problem suffers from a one-sided approach to the child who is to be educated, and from an equally one-sided lack of emphasis on the uneducatedness of the educator. Everyone who has finished his course of studies feels himself to be fully educated; in a word, he feels grown up. He must feel this, he must have this solid conviction of his own competence in order to survive the struggle for existence. Any doubt or feeling of uncertainty would hinder and cripple him, undermining the necessary faith in his own authority and unfitting him for a professional career. People expect him to be efficient and good at his job and not to have doubts about himself and his capabilities. The professional man is irretrievably condemned to be competent.

285   Everyone knows that these conditions are not ideal. But, with reservations, we can say that they are the best possible under the circumstances. We cannot imagine how they could be different. We cannot expect more from the average educator than from the average parent. If he is good at his job, we have to be content with that, just as we have to be content with parents bringing up their children as best they can.

286   The fact is that the high ideal of educating the personality is not for children: for what is usually meant by personality—a well-rounded psychic whole that is capable of resistance and abounding in energy—is an *adult ideal*. It is only in an age like ours, when the individual is unconscious of the problems of adult life, or—what is worse—when he consciously shirks them, that people could wish to foist this ideal on to childhood. I suspect our contemporary pedagogical and psychological enthusiasm for the child of dishonourable intentions: we talk about the child, but we should mean the child in the adult. For in every

adult there lurks a child—an eternal child,[4] something that is always becoming, is never completed, and calls for unceasing care, attention, and education. That is the part of the human personality which wants to develop and become whole. But the man of today is far indeed from this wholeness. Dimly suspecting his own deficiencies, he seizes upon child education and fervently devotes himself to child psychology, fondly supposing that something must have gone wrong in his own upbringing and childhood development that can be weeded out in the next generation. This intention is highly commendable, but comes to grief on the psychological fact that we cannot correct in a child a fault that we ourselves still commit. Children are not half as stupid as we imagine. They notice only too well what is genuine and what is not. Hans Andersen's story of the emperor's clothes contains a perennial truth. How many parents have come to me with the laudable intention of sparing their children the unhappy experiences they had to go through in their own childhood! And when I ask, "Are you quite sure you have overcome these mistakes yourself?" they are firmly convinced that the damage has long since been repaired. In actual fact it has not. If as children they were brought up too strictly, then they spoil their own children with a tolerance bordering on bad taste; if certain matters were painfully concealed from them in childhood, these are revealed with a lack of reticence that is just as painful. They have merely gone to the opposite extreme, the strongest evidence for the tragic survival of the old sin—a fact which has altogether escaped them.

287   If there is anything that we wish to change in our children, we should first examine it and see whether it is not something that could better be changed in ourselves. Take our enthusiasm for pedagogics. It may be that the boot is on the other leg. It may be that we misplace the pedagogical need because it would be an uncomfortable reminder that we ourselves are still children in many respects and still need a vast amount of educating.

288   At any rate this doubt seems to me to be extremely pertinent when we set out to train our children's "personalities." Per-

4 [Cf. C. Kerényi, "The Primordial Child in Primordial Times" and Jung, "The Psychology of the Child-Archetype," in *Essays on a Science of Mythology* (Bollingen Series XXII, New York, 1949; British edition: *Introduction to a Science of Mythology*, London, 1950).—EDITORS.]

sonality is a seed that can only develop by slow stages throughout life. There is no personality without definiteness, wholeness, and ripeness. These three qualities cannot and should not be expected of the child, as they would rob it of childhood. It would be nothing but an abortion, a premature pseudo-adult; yet our modern education has already given birth to such monsters, particularly in those cases where parents set themselves the fanatical task of always "doing their best" for the children and "living only for them." This clamant ideal effectively prevents the parents from doing anything about their own development and allows them to thrust their "best" down their children's throats. This so-called "best" turns out to be the very things the parents have most badly neglected in themselves. In this way the children are goaded on to achieve their parents' most dismal failures, and are loaded with ambitions that are never fulfilled. Such methods and ideals only engender educational monstrosities.

289   No one can train the personality unless he has it himself. And it is not the child, but only the adult, who can achieve personality as the fruit of a full life directed to this end. The achievement of personality means nothing less than the optimum development of the whole individual human being. It is impossible to foresee the endless variety of conditions that have to be fulfilled. A whole lifetime, in all its biological, social, and spiritual aspects, is needed. Personality is the supreme realization of the innate idiosyncrasy of a living being. It is an act of high courage flung in the face of life, the absolute affirmation of all that constitutes the individual, the most successful adaptation to the universal conditions of existence coupled with the greatest possible freedom for self-determination. To educate a man to *this* seems to me no light matter. It is surely the hardest task the modern mind has set itself. And it is dangerous too, dangerous to a degree that Schiller never imagined, though his prophetic insight made him the first to venture upon these problems. It is as dangerous as the bold and hazardous undertaking of nature to let women bear children. Would it not be sacrilege, a Promethean or even Luciferian act of presumption, if a superman ventured to grow an homunculus in a bottle and then found it sprouting into a Golem? And yet he would not be doing anything that nature does not do every day. There is

no human horror or fairground freak that has not lain in the womb of a loving mother. As the sun shines upon the just and the unjust, and as women who bear and give suck tend God's children and the devil's brood with equal compassion, unconcerned about the possible consequences, so we also are part and parcel of this amazing nature, and, like it, carry within us the seeds of the unpredictable.

290   Our personality develops in the course of our life from germs that are hard or impossible to discern, and it is only our deeds that reveal who we are. We are like the sun, which nourishes the life of the earth and brings forth every kind of strange, wonderful, and evil thing; we are like the mothers who bear in their wombs untold happiness and suffering. At first we do not know what deeds or misdeeds, what destiny, what good and evil we have in us, and only the autumn can show what the spring has engendered, only in the evening will it be seen what the morning began.

291   Personality, as the complete realization of our whole being, is an unattainable ideal. But unattainability is no argument against the ideal, for ideals are only signposts, never the goal.

292   Just as the child must develop in order to be educated, so the personality must begin to sprout before it can be trained. And this is where the danger begins. For we are handling something unpredictable, we do not know how and in what direction the budding personality will develop, and we have learned enough of nature and the world to be somewhat chary of both. On top of that, we were brought up in the Christian belief that human nature is intrinsically evil. But even those who no longer adhere to the Christian teaching are by nature mistrustful and not a little frightened of the possibilities lurking in the subterranean chambers of their being. Even enlightened psychologists like Freud give us an extremely unpleasant picture of what lies slumbering in the depths of the human psyche. So it is rather a bold venture to put in a good word for the development of personality. Human nature, however, is full of the strangest contradictions. We praise the "sanctity of motherhood," yet would never dream of holding it responsible for all the human monsters, the homicidal maniacs, dangerous lunatics, epileptics, idiots and cripples of every description who are born every day. At the same time we are tortured with doubts when it comes to

allowing the free development of personality. "Anything might happen then," people say. Or they dish up the old, feeble-minded objection to "individualism." But individualism is not and never has been a natural development; it is nothing but an unnatural usurpation, a freakish, impertinent pose that proves its hollowness by crumpling up before the least obstacle. What we have in mind is something very different.

293   Clearly, no one develops his personality because somebody tells him that it would be useful or advisable to do so. Nature has never yet been taken in by well-meaning advice. The only thing that moves nature is causal necessity, and that goes for human nature too. Without necessity nothing budges, the human personality least of all. It is tremendously conservative, not to say torpid. Only acute necessity is able to rouse it. The developing personality obeys no caprice, no command, no insight, only brute necessity; it needs the motivating force of inner or outer fatalities. Any other development would be no better than individualism. That is why the cry of "individualism" is a cheap insult when flung at the natural development of personality.

294   The words "many are called, but few are chosen" are singularly appropriate here, for the development of personality from the germ-state to full consciousness is at once a charisma and a curse, because its first fruit is the conscious and unavoidable segregation of the single individual from the undifferentiated and unconscious herd. This means isolation, and there is no more comforting word for it. Neither family nor society nor position can save him from this fate, nor yet the most successful adaptation to his environment, however smoothly he fits in. The development of personality is a favour that must be paid for dearly. But the people who talk most loudly about developing their personalities are the very ones who are least mindful of the results, which are such as to frighten away all weaker spirits.

295   Yet the development of personality means more than just the fear of hatching forth monsters, or of isolation. It also means fidelity to the law of one's own being.

296   For the word "fidelity" I should prefer, in this context, the Greek word used in the New Testament, πίστις, which is erroneously translated "faith." It really means "trust," "trustful loyalty."

Fidelity to the law of one's own being is a trust in this law, a
loyal perseverance and confident hope; in short, an attitude
such as a religious man should have towards God. It can now be
seen how portentous is the dilemma that emerges from behind
our problem: personality can never develop unless the individual chooses his own way, consciously and with moral deliberation. Not only the causal motive—necessity—but conscious moral
decision must lend its strength to the process of building the
personality. If the first is lacking, then the alleged development
is a mere acrobatics of the will; if the second, it will get stuck
in unconscious automatism. But a man can make a moral decision to go his own way only if he holds that way to be the
best. If any other way were held to be better, then he would live
and develop that other personality instead of his own. The other
ways are conventionalities of a moral, social, political, philosophical, or religious nature. The fact that the conventions always flourish in one form or another only proves that the vast
majority of mankind do not choose their own way, but convention, and consequently develop not themselves but a method
and a collective mode of life at the cost of their own wholeness.

297   Just as the psychic and social life of mankind at the primitive
level is exclusively a group life with a high degree of unconsciousness among the individuals composing it, so the historical
process of development that comes afterwards is in the main
collective and will doubtless remain so. That is why I believe
convention to be a collective necessity. It is a stopgap and not
an ideal, either in the moral or in the religious sense, for submission to it always means renouncing one's wholeness and
running away from the final consequences of one's own being.

298   To develop one's own personality is indeed an unpopular
undertaking, a deviation that is highly uncongenial to the herd,
an eccentricity smelling of the cenobite, as it seems to the out-
sider. Small wonder, then, that from earliest times only the
chosen few have embarked upon this strange adventure. Had
they all been fools, we could safely dismiss them as ἰδιῶται,
mentally "private" persons who have no claim on our interest.
But, unfortunately, these personalities are as a rule the legendary
heroes of mankind, the very ones who are looked up to, loved,
and worshipped, the true sons of God whose names perish not.
They are the flower and the fruit, the ever fertile seeds of the

tree of humanity. This allusion to historical personalities makes it abundantly clear why the development of personality is an ideal, and why the cry of individualism is an insult. Their greatness has never lain in their abject submission *to* convention, but, on the contrary, in their deliverance *from* convention. They towered up like mountain peaks above the mass that still clung to its collective fears, its beliefs, laws, and systems, and boldly chose their own way. To the man in the street it has always seemed miraculous that anyone should turn aside from the beaten track with its known destinations, and strike out on the steep and narrow path leading into the unknown. Hence it was always believed that such a man, if not actually crazy, was possessed by a daemon or a god; for the miracle of a man being able to act otherwise than as humanity has always acted could only be explained by the gift of daemonic power or divine spirit. How could anyone but a god counterbalance the dead weight of humanity in the mass, with its everlasting convention and habit? From the beginning, therefore, the heroes were endowed with godlike attributes. According to the Nordic view they had snake's eyes, and there was something peculiar about their birth or descent; certain heroes of ancient Greece were snake-souled, others had a personal daemon, were magicians or the elect of God. All these attributes, which could be multiplied at will, show that for the ordinary man the outstanding personality is something *supernatural,* a phenomenon that can only be explained by the intervention of some daemonic factor.

299   What is it, in the end, that induces a man to go his own way and to rise out of unconscious identity with the mass as out of a swathing mist? Not necessity, for necessity comes to many, and they all take refuge in convention. Not moral decision, for nine times out of ten we decide for convention likewise. What is it, then, that inexorably tips the scales in favour of the *extra-ordinary?*

300   It is what is commonly called *vocation:* an irrational factor that destines a man to emancipate himself from the herd and from its well-worn paths. True personality is always a vocation and puts its trust in it as in God, despite its being, as the ordinary man would say, only a personal feeling. But vocation acts like a law of God from which there is no escape. The fact that many a man who goes his own way ends in ruin means nothing to one

who has a vocation. He *must* obey his own law, as if it were a daemon whispering to him of new and wonderful paths. Anyone with a vocation hears the voice of the inner man: he is *called*. That is why the legends say that he possesses a private daemon who counsels him and whose mandates he must obey. The best known example of this is Faust, and an historical instance is provided by the daemon of Socrates. Primitive medicine-men have their snake spirits, and Aesculapius, the tutelary patron of physicians, has for his emblem the Serpent of Epidaurus. He also had, as his private daemon, the Cabir Telesphoros, who is said to have dictated or inspired his medical prescriptions.

301   The original meaning of "to have a vocation" is "to be addressed by a voice." The clearest examples of this are to be found in the avowals of the Old Testament prophets. That it is not just a quaint old-fashioned way of speaking is proved by the confessions of historical personalities such as Goethe and Napoleon, to mention only two familiar examples, who made no secret of their feeling of vocation.

302   Vocation, or the feeling of it, is not, however, the prerogative of great personalities; it is also appropriate to the small ones all the way down to the "midget" personalities, but as the size decreases the voice becomes more and more muffled and unconscious. It is as if the voice of the daemon within were moving further and further off, and spoke more rarely and more indistinctly. The smaller the personality, the dimmer and more unconscious it becomes, until finally it merges indistinguishably with the surrounding society, thus surrendering its own wholeness and dissolving into the wholeness of the group. In the place of the inner voice there is the voice of the group with its conventions, and vocation is replaced by collective necessities. But even in this unconscious social condition there are not a few who are called awake by the summons of the voice, whereupon they are at once set apart from the others, feeling themselves confronted with a problem about which the others know nothing. In most cases it is impossible to explain to the others what has happened, for any understanding is walled off by impenetrable prejudices. "You are no different from anybody else," they will chorus, or, "there's no such thing," and even if there is such a thing, it is immediately branded as "morbid" and

"most unseemly." For it is "a monstrous presumption to suppose anything of that sort could be of the slightest significance"— it is "purely psychological." This last objection is extremely popular nowadays. It stems from a curious underestimation of anything psychic, which people apparently regard as personal, arbitrary, and therefore completely futile. And this, paradoxically enough, despite their enthusiasm for psychology. The unconscious, after all, is "nothing but fantasy." We "merely imagined" so and so, etc. People think themselves magicians who can conjure the psyche hither and thither and fashion it to suit their moods. They deny what strikes them as inconvenient, sublimate anything nasty, explain away their phobias, correct their faults, and feel in the end that they have arranged everything beautifully. In the meantime they have forgotten the essential point, which is that only the tiniest fraction of the psyche is identical with the conscious mind and its box of magic tricks, while for much the greater part it is sheer unconscious *fact,* hard and immitigable as granite, immovable, inaccessible, yet ready at any time to come crashing down upon us at the behest of unseen powers. The gigantic catastrophes that threaten us today are not elemental happenings of a physical or biological order, but psychic events. To a quite terrifying degree we are threatened by wars and revolutions which are nothing other than psychic epidemics. At any moment several millions of human beings may be smitten with a new madness, and then we shall have another world war or devastating revolution. Instead of being at the mercy of wild beasts, earthquakes, landslides, and inundations, modern man is battered by the elemental forces of his own psyche. This is the World Power that vastly exceeds all other powers on earth. The Age of Enlightenment, which stripped nature and human institutions of gods, overlooked the God of Terror who dwells in the human soul. If anywhere, fear of God is justified in face of the overwhelming supremacy of the psychic.

303   But all this is so much abstraction. Everyone knows that the intellect, that clever jackanapes, can put it this way or any other way he pleases. It is a very different thing when the psyche, as an objective fact, hard as granite and heavy as lead, confronts a man as an inner experience and addresses him in an audible voice, saying, "This is what will and must be." Then he feels

himself called, just as the group does when there's a war on, or a revolution, or any other madness. It is not for nothing that our age calls for the redeemer personality, for the one who can emancipate himself from the inescapable grip of the collective and save at least his own soul, who lights a beacon of hope for others, proclaiming that here is at least *one* man who has succeeded in extricating himself from that fatal identity with the group psyche. For the group, because of its unconsciousness, has no freedom of choice, and so psychic activity runs on in it like an uncontrolled law of nature. There is thus set going a chain reaction that comes to a stop only in catastrophe. The people always long for a hero, a slayer of dragons, when they feel the danger of psychic forces; hence the cry for personality.

304   But what has the individual personality to do with the plight of the many? In the first place he is part of the people as a whole, and is as much at the mercy of the power that moves the whole as anybody else. The only thing that distinguishes him from all the others is his vocation. He has been called by that all-powerful, all-tyrannizing psychic necessity that is his own and his people's affliction. If he hearkens to the voice, he is at once set apart and isolated, as he has resolved to obey the law that commands him from within. "His *own* law!" everybody will cry. But he knows better: it is *the* law, *the* vocation for which he is destined, no more "his own" than the lion that fells him, although it is undoubtedly this particular lion that kills him and not any other lion. Only in this sense is he entitled to speak of "his" vocation, "his" law.

305   With the decision to put his way above all other possible ways he has already fulfilled the greater part of his vocation as a redeemer. He has invalidated all other ways for himself, exalting his law above convention and thus making a clean sweep of all those things that not only failed to prevent the great danger but actually accelerated it. For conventions in themselves are soulless mechanisms that can never understand more than the mere routine of life. Creative life always stands outside convention. That is why, when the mere routine of life predominates in the form of convention and tradition, there is bound to be a destructive outbreak of creative energy. This outbreak is a catastrophe only when it is a mass phenomenon, but never in the individual who consciously submits to these higher powers

and serves them with all his strength. The mechanism of convention keeps people unconscious, for in that state they can follow their accustomed tracks like blind brutes, without the need for conscious decision. This unintended result of even the best conventions is unavoidable but is no less a terrible danger for that. For when new conditions arise that are not provided for under the old conventions, then, just as with animals, panic is liable to break out among human beings kept unconscious by routine, and with equally unpredictable results.

306 Personality, however, does not allow itself to be seized by the panic terror of those who are just waking to consciousness, for it has put all its terrors behind it. It is able to cope with the changing times, and has unknowingly and involuntarily become a *leader*.

307 All human beings are much alike, otherwise they could not succumb to the same delusion, and the psychic substratum upon which the individual consciousness is based is universally the same, otherwise people could never reach a common understanding. So, in this sense, personality and its peculiar psychic make-up are not something absolutely unique. The uniqueness holds only for the *individual* nature of the personality, as it does for each and every individual. To become a personality is not the absolute prerogative of the genius, for a man may be a genius without being a personality. In so far as every individual has the law of his life inborn in him, it is theoretically possible for any man to follow this law and so become a personality, that is, to achieve wholeness. But since life only exists in the form of living units, i.e., individuals, the law of life always tends towards a life individually lived. So although the objective psyche can only be conceived as a universal and uniform datum, which means that all men share the same primary, psychic condition, this objective psyche must nevertheless individuate itself if it is to become actualized, for there is no other way in which it could express itself except through the individual human being. The only exception to this is when it seizes hold of a group, in which case it must, of its own nature, precipitate a catastrophe, because it can only operate unconsciously and is not assimilated by any consciousness or assigned its place among the existing conditions of life.

308   Only the man who can consciously assent to the power of the inner voice becomes a personality; but if he succumbs to it he will be swept away by the blind flux of psychic events and destroyed. That is the great and liberating thing about any genuine personality: he voluntarily sacrifices himself to his vocation, and consciously translates into his own individual reality what would only lead to ruin if it were lived unconsciously by the group.

309   One of the most shining examples of the meaning of personality that history has preserved for us is the life of Christ. In Christianity, which, be it mentioned in passing, was the only religion really persecuted by the Romans, there rose up a direct opponent of the Caesarean madness that afflicted not only the emperor, but every Roman as well: *civis Romanus sum.* The opposition showed itself wherever the worship of Caesar clashed with Christianity. But, as we know from what the evangelists tell us about the psychic development of Christ's personality, this opposition was fought out just as decisively in the soul of its founder. The story of the Temptation clearly reveals the nature of the psychic power with which Jesus came into collision: it was the power-intoxicated devil of the prevailing Caesarean psychology that led him into dire temptation in the wilderness. This devil was the objective psyche that held all the peoples of the Roman Empire under its sway, and that is why it promised Jesus all the kingdoms of the earth, as if it were trying to make a Caesar of him. Obeying the inner call of his vocation, Jesus voluntarily exposed himself to the assaults of the imperialistic madness that filled everyone, conqueror and conquered alike. In this way he recognized the nature of the objective psyche which had plunged the whole world into misery and had begotten a yearning for salvation that found expression even in the pagan poets. Far from suppressing or allowing himself to be suppressed by this psychic onslaught, he let it act on him consciously, and assimilated it. Thus was world-conquering Caesarism transformed into spiritual kingship, and the Roman Empire into the universal kingdom of God that was not of this world. While the whole Jewish nation was expecting an imperialistically minded and politically active hero as a Messiah, Jesus fulfilled the Messianic mission not so much for his own nation as for the whole Roman world, and pointed out to hu-

manity the old truth that where force rules there is no love, and where love reigns force does not count. The religion of love was the exact psychological counterpart to the Roman devil-worship of power.

310   The example of Christianity is perhaps the best illustration of my previous abstract argument. This apparently unique life became a sacred symbol because it is the psychological prototype of the only meaningful life, that is, of a life that strives for the individual realization—absolute and unconditional—of its own particular law. Well may we exclaim with Tertullian: *anima naturaliter christiana!*

311   The deification of Jesus, as also of the Buddha, is not surprising, for it affords a striking example of the enormous valuation that humanity places upon these hero figures and hence upon the ideal of personality. Though it seems at present as if the blind and destructive dominance of meaningless collective forces would thrust the ideal of personality into the background, yet this is only a passing revolt against the dead weight of history. Once the revolutionary, unhistorical, and therefore uneducated inclinations of the rising generation have had their fill of tearing down tradition, new heroes will be sought and found. Even the Bolsheviks, whose radicalism leaves nothing to be desired, have embalmed Lenin and made a saviour of Karl Marx. The ideal of personality is one of the ineradicable needs of the human soul, and the more unsuitable it is the more fanatically it is defended. Indeed, the worship of Caesar was itself a misconceived cult of personality, and modern Protestantism, whose critical theology has reduced the divinity of Christ to vanishing point, has found its last refuge in the personality of Jesus.

312   Yes, this thing we call personality is a great and mysterious problem. Everything that can be said about it is curiously unsatisfactory and inadequate, and there is always a danger of the discussion losing itself in pomposity and empty chatter. The very idea of personality is, in common usage, so vague and ill-defined that one hardly ever finds two people who take the word in the same sense. If I put forward a more definite conception of it, I do not imagine that I have uttered the last word. I should like to regard all I say here only as a tentative attempt to approach the problem of personality without making any claim to solve it. Or rather, I should like my attempt to be regarded

181

as a description of the psychological problems raised by personality. All the usual explanations and nostrums of psychology are apt to fall short here, just as they do with the man of genius or the creative artist. Inferences from heredity or from environment do not quite come off; inventing fictions about childhood, so popular today, ends—to put it mildly—in unreality; explanations from necessity—"he had no money," "he was a sick man," etc.—remain caught in externals. There is always something irrational to be added, something that simply cannot be explained, a *deus ex machina* or an *asylum ignorantiae,* that well-known sobriquet for God. The problem thus seems to border on the extrahuman realm, which has always been known by a divine name. As you can see, I too have had to refer to the "inner voice," the vocation, and define it as a powerful objective-psychic factor in order to characterize the way in which it functions in the developing personality and how it appears subjectively. Mephistopheles, in *Faust,* is not personified merely because this creates a better dramatic or theatrical effect, as though Faust were his own moralist and painted his private devil on the wall. The opening words of the Dedication—"Once more you hover near me, forms and faces"—are more than just an aesthetic flourish. Like the concretism of the devil, they are an admission of the objectivity of psychic experience, a whispered avowal that this was what *actually happened,* not because of subjective wishes, or fears, or personal opinions, but somehow quite of itself. Naturally only a numskull thinks of ghosts, but something like a primitive numskull seems to lurk beneath the surface of our reasonable daytime consciousness.

313   Hence the eternal doubt whether what appears to be the objective psyche is really objective, or whether it might not be imagination after all. But then the question at once arises: have I imagined such and such a thing on purpose, or has it been imagined by something in me? It is a similar problem to that of the neurotic who suffers from an imaginary carcinoma. He knows, and has been told a hundred times before, that it is all imagination, and yet he asks me brokenly, "But why do I imagine such a thing? I don't want to do it!" To which the answer is: the idea of the carcinoma has imagined itself in him without his knowledge and without his consent. The reason is that a psychic growth, a "proliferation," is taking place in his uncon-

scious without his being able to make it conscious. In the face of this interior activity he feels afraid. But since he is entirely persuaded that there can be nothing in his own soul that he does not know about, he must relate his fear to a physical carcinoma which he knows does not exist. And if he should still be afraid of it, there are a hundred doctors to convince him that his fear is entirely groundless. The neurosis is thus a defence against the objective, inner activity of the psyche, or an attempt, somewhat dearly paid for, to escape from the inner voice and hence from the vocation. For this "growth" is the objective activity of the psyche, which, independently of conscious volition, is trying to speak to the conscious mind through the inner voice and lead him towards wholeness. Behind the neurotic perversion is concealed his vocation, his destiny: the growth of personality, the full realization of the life-will that is born with the individual. It is the man without *amor fati* who is the neurotic; he, truly, has missed his vocation, and never will he be able to say with Cromwell, "None climbeth so high as he who knoweth not whither his destiny leadeth him." [5]

314   To the extent that a man is untrue to the law of his being and does not rise to personality, he has failed to realize his life's meaning. Fortunately, in her kindness and patience, Nature never puts the fatal question as to the meaning of their lives into the mouths of most people. And where no one asks, no one need answer.

315   The neurotic's fear of carcinoma is therefore justified: it is not imagination, but the consistent expression of a psychic fact that exists in a sphere outside consciousness, beyond the reach of his will and understanding. If he withdrew into the wilderness and listened to his inner life in solitude, he might perhaps hear what the voice has to say. But as a rule the miseducated, civilized human being is quite incapable of perceiving the voice, which is something not guaranteed by the current shibboleths. Primitive people have a far greater capacity in this respect; at least the medicine-men are able, as part of their professional equipment, to talk with spirits, trees, and animals, these being the forms in which they encounter the objective psyche or psychic non-ego.

5 [In the German, attributed to Nietzsche.—EDITORS.]

316   Because neurosis is a developmental disturbance of the personality, we physicians of the soul are compelled by professional necessity to concern ourselves with the problem of personality and the inner voice, however remote it may seem to be. In practical psychotherapy these psychic facts, which are usually so vague and have so often degenerated into empty phrases, emerge from obscurity and take visible shape. Nevertheless, it is extremely rare for this to happen spontaneously as it did with the Old Testament prophets; generally the psychic conditions that have caused the disturbance have to be made conscious with considerable effort. But the contents that then come to light are wholly in accord with the inner voice and point to a predestined vocation, which, if accepted and assimilated by the conscious mind, conduces to the development of personality.

317   Just as the great personality acts upon society to liberate, to redeem, to transform, and to heal, so the birth of personality in oneself has a therapeutic effect. It is as if a river that had run to waste in sluggish side-streams and marshes suddenly found its way back to its proper bed, or as if a stone lying on a germinating seed were lifted away so that the shoot could begin its natural growth.

318   The inner voice is the voice of a fuller life, of a wider, more comprehensive consciousness. That is why, in mythology, the birth of the hero or the symbolic rebirth coincides with sunrise, for the growth of personality is synonymous with an increase of self-consciousness. For the same reason most heroes are characterized by solar attributes, and the moment of birth of their greater personality is known as illumination.

319   The fear that most people naturally have of the inner voice is not so childish as might be supposed. The contents that rise up and confront a limited consciousness are far from harmless, as is shown by the classic example of the temptation of Christ, or the equally significant Mara episode in the Buddha legend. As a rule, they signify the specific danger to which the person concerned is liable to succumb. What the inner voice whispers to us is generally something negative, if not actually evil. This must be so, first of all because we are usually not as unconscious of our virtues as of our vices, and then because we suffer less from the good than from the bad in us. The inner voice, as I have explained above, makes us conscious of the evil from which the

whole community is suffering, whether it be the nation or the whole human race. But it presents this evil in an individual form, so that one might at first suppose it to be only an individual characteristic. The inner voice brings the evil before us in a very tempting and convincing way in order to make us succumb. If we do not partially succumb, nothing of this apparent evil enters into us, and no regeneration or healing can take place. (I say "apparent," though this may sound too optimistic.) If we succumb completely, then the contents expressed by the inner voice act as so many devils, and a catastrophe ensues. But if we can succumb only in part, and if by self-assertion the ego can save itself from being completely swallowed, then it can assimilate the voice, and we realize that the evil was, after all, only a semblance of evil, but in reality a bringer of healing and illumination. In fact, the inner voice is a "Lucifer" in the strictest and most unequivocal sense of the word, and it faces people with ultimate moral decisions without which they can never achieve full consciousness and become personalities. The highest and the lowest, the best and the vilest, the truest and the most deceptive things are often blended together in the inner voice in the most baffling way, thus opening up in us an abyss of confusion, falsehood, and despair.

320   It is naturally absurd for people to accuse the voice of Nature, the all-sustainer and all-destroyer, of evil. If she appears inveterately evil to us, this is mainly due to the old truth that the good is always the enemy of the better. We would be foolish indeed if we did not cling to the traditional good for as long as possible. But as Faust says:

> When we the good things of this world attain
> We call the better all a lie and sham.

A good thing is unfortunately not a good forever, for otherwise there would be nothing better. If better is to come, good must stand aside. Therefore Meister Eckhart says, "God is not good, or else he could be better."

321   There are times in the world's history—and our own time may be one of them—when good must stand aside, so that anything destined to be better first appears in evil form. This shows how extremely dangerous it is even to touch these problems, for evil can so easily slip in on the plea that it is, potentially, the

better! The problems of the inner voice are full of pitfalls and hidden snares. Treacherous, slippery ground, as dangerous and pathless as life itself once one lets go of the railings. But he who cannot lose his life, neither shall he save it. The hero's birth and the heroic life are always threatened. The serpents sent by Hera to destroy the infant Hercules, the python that tries to strangle Apollo at birth, the massacre of the innocents, all these tell the same story. To develop the personality is a gamble, and the tragedy is that the daemon of the inner voice is at once our greatest danger and an indispensable help. It is tragic, but logical, for it is the nature of things to be so.

322   Can we, therefore, blame humanity, and all the well-meaning shepherds of the flock and worried fathers of families, if they erect protective barriers, hold up wonder-working images, and point out the roads that wind safely past the abyss?

323   But, in the end, the hero, the leader, the saviour, is one who discovers a new way to greater certainty. Everything could be left undisturbed did not the new way demand to be discovered, and did it not visit humanity with all the plagues of Egypt until it finally is discovered. The undiscovered vein within us is a living part of the psyche; classical Chinese philosophy names this interior way "Tao," and likens it to a flow of water that moves irresistibly towards its goal. To rest in Tao means fulfilment, wholeness, one's destination reached, one's mission done; the beginning, end, and perfect realization of the meaning of existence innate in all things. Personality is Tao.

VIII

MARRIAGE AS A PSYCHOLOGICAL RELATIONSHIP

MARRIAGE AS A PSYCHOLOGICAL RELATIONSHIP [1]

324   Regarded as a psychological relationship, marriage is a highly complex structure made up of a whole series of subjective and objective factors, mostly of a very heterogeneous nature. As I wish to confine myself here to the purely psychological problems of marriage, I must disregard in the main the objective factors of a legal and social nature, although these cannot fail to have a pronounced influence on the psychological relationship between the marriage partners.

325   Whenever we speak of a "psychological relationship" we presuppose one that is *conscious*, for there is no such thing as a psychological relationship between two people who are in a state of unconsciousness. From the psychological point of view they would be wholly without relationship. From any other point of view, the physiological for example, they could be regarded as related, but one could not call their relationship psychological. It must be admitted that though such total unconsciousness as I have assumed does not occur, there is nevertheless a not inconsiderable degree of partial unconsciousness, and the psychological relationship is limited in the degree to which that unconsciousness exists.

1 [First published as "Die Ehe als psychologische Beziehung," in *Das Ehebuch* (Celle, 1925), a volume edited by Count Hermann Keyserling; translated by Theresa Duerr in the English version, *The Book of Marriage* (New York, 1926). The original was reprinted in *Seelenprobleme der Gegenwart* (Zurich, 1931). The essay was again translated into English by H. G. and Cary F. Baynes in *Contributions to Analytical Psychology* (London and New York, 1928), and this version has been freely consulted in the present translation.—EDITORS.]

326   In the child, consciousness rises out of the depths of unconscious psychic life, at first like separate islands, which gradually unite to form a "continent," a continuous land-mass of consciousness. Progressive mental development means, in effect, extension of consciousness. With the rise of a continuous consciousness, and not before, psychological relationship becomes possible. So far as we know, consciousness is always ego-consciousness. In order to be conscious of myself, I must be able to distinguish myself from others. Relationship can only take place where this distinction exists. But although the distinction may be made in a general way, normally it is incomplete, because large areas of psychic life still remain unconscious. As no distinction can be made with regard to unconscious contents, on this terrain no relationship can be established; here there still reigns the original unconscious condition of the ego's primitive identity with others, in other words a complete absence of relationship.

327   The young person of marriageable age does, of course, possess an ego-consciousness (girls more than men, as a rule), but, since he has only recently emerged from the mists of original unconsciousness, he is certain to have wide areas which still lie in the shadow and which preclude to that extent the formation of psychological relationship. This means, in practice, that the young man (or woman) can have only an incomplete understanding of himself and others, and is therefore imperfectly informed as to his, and their, motives. As a rule the motives he acts from are largely unconscious. Subjectively, of course, he thinks himself very conscious and knowing, for we constantly overestimate the existing content of consciousness, and it is a great and surprising discovery when we find that what we had supposed to be the final peak is nothing but the first step in a very long climb. The greater the area of unconsciousness, the less is marriage a matter of free choice, as is shown subjectively in the fatal compulsion one feels so acutely when one is in love. The compulsion can exist even when one is not in love, though in less agreeable form.

328   Unconscious motivations are of a personal and of a general nature. First of all, there are the motives deriving from parental influence. The relationship of the young man to his mother, and of the girl to her father, is the determining factor in this respect.

It is the strength of the bond to the parents that unconsciously influences the choice of husband or wife, either positively or negatively. Conscious love for either parent favours the choice of a like mate, while an unconscious tie (which need not by any means express itself consciously as love) makes the choice difficult and imposes characteristic modifications. In order to understand them, one must know first of all the cause of the unconscious tie to the parents, and under what conditions it forcibly modifies, or even prevents, the conscious choice. Generally speaking, all the life which the parents could have lived, but of which they thwarted themselves for artificial motives, is passed on to the children in substitute form. That is to say, the children are driven unconsciously in a direction that is intended to compensate for everything that was left unfulfilled in the lives of their parents. Hence it is that excessively moral-minded parents have what are called "unmoral" children, or an irresponsible wastrel of a father has a son with a positively morbid amount of ambition, and so on. The worst results flow from parents who have kept themselves artificially unconscious. Take the case of a mother who deliberately keeps herself unconscious so as not to disturb the pretence of a "satisfactory" marriage. Unconsciously she will bind her son to her, more or less as a substitute for a husband. The son, if not forced directly into homosexuality, is compelled to modify his choice in a way that is contrary to his true nature. He may, for instance, marry a girl who is obviously inferior to his mother and therefore unable to compete with her; or he will fall for a woman of a tyrannical and overbearing disposition, who may perhaps succeed in tearing him away from his mother. The choice of a mate, if the instincts have not been vitiated, may remain free from these influences, but sooner or later they will make themselves felt as obstacles. A more or less instinctive choice might be considered the best from the point of view of maintaining the species, but it is not always fortunate psychologically, because there is often an uncommonly large difference between the purely instinctive personality and one that is individually differentiated. And though in such cases the race might be improved and invigorated by a purely instinctive choice, individual happiness would be bound to suffer. (The idea of "instinct" is of course nothing more than a collec-

191

tive term for all kinds of organic and psychic factors whose nature is for the most part unknown.)

329   If the individual is to be regarded solely as an instrument for maintaining the species, then the purely instinctive choice of a mate is by far the best. But since the foundations of such a choice are unconscious, only a kind of impersonal liaison can be built upon them, such as can be observed to perfection among primitives. If we can speak here of a "relationship" at all, it is, at best, only a pale reflection of what we mean, a very distant state of affairs with a decidedly impersonal character, wholly regulated by traditional customs and prejudices, the prototype of every conventional marriage.

330   So far as reason or calculation or the so-called loving care of the parents does not arrange the marriage, and the pristine instincts of the children are not vitiated either by false education or by the hidden influence of accumulated and neglected parental complexes, the marriage choice will normally follow the unconscious motivations of instinct. Unconsciousness results in non-differentiation, or unconscious identity. The practical consequence of this is that one person presupposes in the other a psychological structure similar to his own. Normal sex life, as a shared experience with apparently similar aims, further strengthens the feeling of unity and identity. This state is described as one of complete harmony, and is extolled as a great happiness ("one heart and one soul")—not without good reason, since the return to that original condition of unconscious oneness is like a return to childhood. Hence the childish gestures of all lovers. Even more is it a return to the mother's womb, into the teeming depths of an as yet unconscious creativity. It is, in truth, a genuine and incontestable experience of the Divine, whose transcendent force obliterates and consumes everything individual; a real communion with life and the impersonal power of fate. The individual will for self-possession is broken: the woman becomes the mother, the man the father, and thus both are robbed of their freedom and made instruments of the life urge.

331   Here the relationship remains within the bounds of the biological instinctive goal, the preservation of the species. Since this goal is of a collective nature, the psychological link between husband and wife will also be essentially collective, and cannot

be regarded as an individual relationship in the psychological sense. We can only speak of this when the nature of the unconscious motivations has been recognized and the original identity broken down. Seldom or never does a marriage develop into an individual relationship smoothly and without crises. There is no birth of consciousness without pain.

331a   The ways that lead to conscious realization are many, but they follow definite laws. In general, the change begins with the onset of the second half of life. The middle period of life is a time of enormous psychological importance. The child begins its psychological life within very narrow limits, inside the magic circle of the mother and the family. With progressive maturation it widens its horizon and its own sphere of influence; its hopes and intentions are directed to extending the scope of personal power and possessions; desire reaches out to the world in ever-widening range; the will of the individual becomes more and more identical with the natural goals pursued by unconscious motivations. Thus man breathes his own life into things, until finally they begin to live of themselves and to multiply; and imperceptibly he is overgrown by them. Mothers are overtaken by their children, men by their own creations, and what was originally brought into being only with labour and the greatest effort can no longer be held in check. First it was passion, then it became duty, and finally an intolerable burden, a vampire that battens on the life of its creator. Middle life is the moment of greatest unfolding, when a man still gives himself to his work with his whole strength and his whole will. But in this very moment evening is born, and the second half of life begins. Passion now changes her face and is called duty; "I want" becomes the inexorable "I must," and the turnings of the pathway that once brought surprise and discovery become dulled by custom. The wine has fermented and begins to settle and clear. Conservative tendencies develop if all goes well; instead of looking forward one looks backward, most of the time involuntarily, and one begins to take stock, to see how one's life has developed up to this point. The real motivations are sought and real discoveries are made. The critical survey of himself and his fate enables a man to recognize his peculiarities. But these insights do not come to him easily; they are gained only through the severest shocks.

331b   Since the aims of the second half of life are different from those of the first, to linger too long in the youthful attitude produces a division of the will. Consciousness still presses forward, in obedience, as it were, to its own inertia, but the unconscious lags behind, because the strength and inner resolve needed for further expansion have been sapped. This disunity with oneself begets discontent, and since one is not conscious of the real state of things one generally projects the reasons for it upon one's partner. A critical atmosphere thus develops, the necessary prelude to conscious realization. Usually this state does not begin simultaneously for both partners. Even the best of marriages cannot expunge individual differences so completely that the state of mind of the partners is absolutely identical. In most cases one of them will adapt to marriage more quickly than the other. The one who is grounded on a positive relationship to the parents will find little or no difficulty in adjusting to his or her partner, while the other may be hindered by a deep-seated unconscious tie to the parents. He will therefore achieve complete adaptation only later, and, because it is won with greater difficulty, it may even prove the more durable.

331c   These differences in tempo, and in the degree of spiritual development, are the chief causes of a typical difficulty which makes its appearance at critical moments. In speaking of "the degree of spiritual development" of a personality, I do not wish to imply an especially rich or magnanimous nature. Such is not the case at all. I mean, rather, a certain complexity of mind or nature, comparable to a gem with many facets as opposed to the simple cube. There are many-sided and rather problematical natures burdened with hereditary traits that are sometimes very difficult to reconcile. Adaptation to such natures, or their adaptation to simpler personalities, is always a problem. These people, having a certain tendency to dissociation, generally have the capacity to split off irreconcilable traits of character for considerable periods, thus passing themselves off as much simpler than they are; or it may happen that their many-sidedness, their very versatility, lends them a peculiar charm. Their partners can easily lose themselves in such a labyrinthine nature, finding in it such an abundance of possible experiences that their personal interests are completely absorbed, sometimes in a not very agreeable way, since their sole occupation then consists in tracking the other through all the twists and turns of his character. There is always so much experience available that the simpler personality is surrounded, if not actually swamped, by it; he is swallowed up in his more complex partner and cannot see his way out. It is an almost regular occurrence for a woman to be wholly contained, spiritually, in her husband, and for a husband to be wholly contained, emotionally, in his wife. One could describe this as the problem of the "contained" and the "container."

332   The one who is contained feels himself to be living entirely within the confines of his marriage; his attitude to the marriage partner is undivided; outside the marriage there exist no essential obligations and no binding interests. The unpleasant side of this otherwise ideal partnership is the disquieting dependence upon a personality that can never be seen in its entirety, and is therefore not altogether credible or dependable. The great advantage lies in his own undividedness, and this is a factor not to be underrated in the psychic economy.

333   The container, on the other hand, who in accordance with his tendency to dissociation has an especial need to unify himself in undivided love for another, will be left far behind in this effort, which is naturally very difficult for him, by the simpler personality. While he is seeking in the latter all the subtleties and complexities that would complement and correspond to his own facets, he is disturbing the other's simplicity. Since in normal circumstances simplicity always has the advantage over complexity, he will very soon be obliged to abandon his efforts to arouse subtle and intricate reactions in a simpler nature. And soon enough his partner, who in accordance with her [2] simpler nature expects simple answers from him, will give him plenty to do by constellating his complexities with her everlasting insistence on simple answers. Willynilly, he must withdraw into himself before the suasions of simplicity. Any mental effort, like the conscious process itself, is so much of a strain for the ordinary man that he invariably prefers the simple, even when it does not

[2] [In translating this and the following passages, I have, for the sake of clarity, assumed that the container is the man and the contained the woman. This assumption is due entirely to the exigencies of English grammar, and is not implied in the German text. Needless to say, the situation could just as easily be reversed.—TRANS.]

happen to be the truth. And when it represents at least a half-truth, then it is all up with him. The simpler nature works on the more complicated like a room that is too small, that does not allow him enough space. The complicated nature, on the other hand, gives the simpler one too many rooms with too much space, so that she never knows where she really belongs. So it comes about quite naturally that the more complicated contains the simpler. The former cannot be absorbed in the latter, but encompasses it without being itself contained. Yet, since the more complicated has perhaps a greater need of being contained than the other, he feels himself outside the marriage and accordingly always plays the problematical role. The more the contained clings, the more the container feels shut out of the relationship. The contained pushes into it by her clinging, and the more she pushes, the less the container is able to respond. He therefore tends to spy out of the window, no doubt unconsciously at first; but with the onset of middle age there awakens in him a more insistent longing for that unity and undividedness which is especially necessary to him on account of his dissociated nature. At this juncture things are apt to occur that bring the conflict to a head. He becomes conscious of the fact that he is seeking completion, seeking the contentedness and undividedness that have always been lacking. For the contained this is only a confirmation of the insecurity she has always felt so painfully; she discovers that in the rooms which apparently belonged to her there dwell other, unwished-for guests. The hope of security vanishes, and this disappointment drives her in on herself, unless by desperate and violent efforts she can succeed in forcing her partner to capitulate, and in extorting a confession that his longing for unity was nothing but a childish or morbid fantasy. If these tactics do not succeed, her acceptance of failure may do her a real good, by forcing her to recognize that the security she was so desperately seeking in the other is to be found in herself. In this way she finds herself and discovers in her own simpler nature all those complexities which the container had sought for in vain.

334   If the container does not break down in face of what we are wont to call "unfaithfulness," but goes on believing in the inner justification of his longing for unity, he will have to put up with his self-division for the time being. A dissociation is not healed

by being split off, but by more complete disintegration. All the powers that strive for unity, all healthy desire for selfhood, will resist the disintegration, and in this way he will become conscious of the possibility of an inner integration, which before he had always sought outside himself. He will then find his reward in an undivided self.

335   This is what happens very frequently about the midday of life, and in this wise our miraculous human nature enforces the transition that leads from the first half of life to the second. It is a metamorphosis from a state in which man is only a tool of instinctive nature, to another in which he is no longer a tool, but himself: a transformation of nature into culture, of instinct into spirit.

336   One should take great care not to interrupt this necessary development by acts of moral violence, for any attempt to create a spiritual attitude by splitting off and suppressing the instincts is a falsification. Nothing is more repulsive than a furtively prurient spirituality; it is just as unsavoury as gross sensuality. But the transition takes a long time, and the great majority of people get stuck in the first stages. If only we could, like the primitives, leave the unconscious to look after this whole psychological development which marriage entails, these transformations could be worked out more completely and without too much friction. So often among so-called "primitives" one comes across spiritual personalities who immediately inspire respect, as though they were the fully matured products of an undisturbed fate. I speak here from personal experience. But where among present-day Europeans can one find people not deformed by acts of moral violence? We are still barbarous enough to believe both in asceticism and its opposite. But the wheel of history cannot be put back; we can only strive towards an attitude that will allow us to live out our fate as undisturbedly as the primitive pagan in us really wants. Only on this condition can we be sure of not perverting spirituality into sensuality, and vice versa; for both must live, each drawing life from the other.

337   The transformation I have briefly described above is the very essence of the psychological marriage relationship. Much could be said about the illusions that serve the ends of nature and bring about the transformations that are characteristic of middle life. The peculiar harmony that characterizes mar-

riage during the first half of life—provided the adjustment is successful—is largely based on the projection of certain archetypal images, as the critical phase makes clear.

338   Every man carries within him the eternal image of woman, not the image of this or that particular woman, but a definite feminine image. This image is fundamentally unconscious, an hereditary factor of primordial origin engraved in the living organic system of the man, an imprint or "archetype" of all the ancestral experiences of the female, a deposit, as it were, of all the impressions ever made by woman—in short, an inherited system of psychic adaptation. Even if no women existed, it would still be possible, at any given time, to deduce from this unconscious image exactly how a woman would have to be constituted psychically. The same is true of the woman: she too has her inborn image of man. Actually, we know from experience that it would be more accurate to describe it as an image of *men,* whereas in the case of the man it is rather the image of *woman.* Since this image is unconscious, it is always unconsciously projected upon the person of the beloved, and is one of the chief reasons for passionate attraction or aversion. I have called this image the "anima," and I find the scholastic question *Habet mulier animam?* especially interesting, since in my view it is an intelligent one inasmuch as the doubt seems justified. Woman has no anima, no soul, but she has an *animus.* The anima has an erotic, emotional character, the animus a rationalizing one. Hence most of what men say about feminine eroticism, and particularly about the emotional life of women, is derived from their own anima projections and distorted accordingly. On the other hand, the astonishing assumptions and fantasies that women make about men come from the activity of the animus, who produces an inexhaustible supply of illogical arguments and false explanations.

339   Anima and animus are both characterized by an extraordinary many-sidedness. In a marriage it is always the contained who projects this image upon the container, while the latter is only partially able to project his unconscious image upon his partner. The more unified and simple this partner is, the less complete the projection. In which case, this highly fascinating image hangs as it were in mid air, as though waiting to be filled out by a living person. There are certain types of women who

seem to be made by nature to attract anima projections; indeed one could almost speak of a definite "anima type." The so-called "sphinx-like" character is an indispensable part of their equipment, also an equivocalness, an intriguing elusiveness—not an indefinite blur that offers nothing, but an indefiniteness that seems full of promises, like the speaking silence of a Mona Lisa. A woman of this kind is both old and young, mother and daughter, of more than doubtful chastity, childlike, and yet endowed with a naïve cunning that is extremely disarming to men.[3] Not every man of real intellectual power can be an animus, for the animus must be a master not so much of fine ideas as of fine words—words seemingly full of meaning which purport to leave a great deal unsaid. He must also belong to the "misunderstood" class, or be in some way at odds with his environment, so that the idea of self-sacrifice can insinuate itself. He must be a rather questionable hero, a man with possibilities, which is not to say that an animus projection may not discover a real hero long before he has become perceptible to the sluggish wits of the man of "average intelligence."[4]

340   For man as well as for woman, in so far as they are "containers," the filling out of this image is an experience fraught with consequences, for it holds the possibility of finding one's own complexities answered by a corresponding diversity. Wide vistas seem to open up in which one feels oneself embraced and contained. I say "seem" advisedly, because the experience may be two-faced. Just as the animus projection of a woman can often pick on a man of real significance who is not recognized by the mass, and can actually help him to achieve his true destiny with her moral support, so a man can create for himself a *femme inspiratrice* by his anima projection. But more often it turns out to be an illusion with destructive consequences, a failure because his faith was not sufficiently strong. To the pessimists I would say that these primordial psychic images have an extraordinarily positive value, but I must warn the optimists against

[3] There are excellent descriptions of this type in H. Rider Haggard's *She* (London, 1887) and Pierre Benoît's *L'Atlantide* (Paris, 1920; trans. by Mary C. Tongue and Mary Ross as *Atlantida*, New York, 1920).

[4] A passably good account of the animus is to be found in Marie Hay's book *The Evil Vineyard* (New York, 1923), also in Elinor Wylie's *Jennifer Lorn* (New York, 1923) and Selma Lagerlöf's *Gösta Berlings Saga* (1891; English trans. by P. B. Flach, *The Story of Gösta Berling*, 1898).

blinding fantasies and the likelihood of the most absurd aberrations.

341   One should on no account take this projection for an individual and conscious relationship. In its first stages it is far from that, for it creates a compulsive dependence based on unconscious motives other than the biological ones. Rider Haggard's *She* gives some indication of the curious world of ideas that underlies the anima projection. They are in essence spiritual contents, often in erotic disguise, obvious fragments of a primitive mythological mentality that consists of archetypes, and whose totality constitutes the collective unconscious. Accordingly, such a relationship is at bottom collective and not individual. (Benoît, who created in *L'Atlantide* a fantasy figure similar even in details to "She," denies having plagiarized Rider Haggard.)

342   If such a projection fastens on to one of the marriage partners, a collective spiritual relationship conflicts with the collective biological one and produces in the container the division or disintegration I have described above. If he is able to hold his head above water, he will find himself through this very conflict. In that case the projection, though dangerous in itself, will have helped him to pass from a collective to an individual relationship. This amounts to full conscious realization of the relationship that marriage brings. Since the aim of this paper is a discussion of the psychology of marriage, the psychology of projection cannot concern us here. It is sufficient to mention it as a fact.

343   One can hardly deal with the psychological marriage relationship without mentioning, even at the risk of misunderstanding, the nature of its critical transitions. As is well known, one understands nothing psychological unless one has experienced it oneself. Not that this ever prevents anyone from feeling convinced that his own judgment is the only true and competent one. This disconcerting fact comes from the necessary overvaluation of the momentary content of consciousness, for without this concentration of attention one could not be conscious at all. Thus it is that every period of life has its own psychological truth, and the same applies to every stage of psychological development. There are even stages which only the few can reach, it being a question of race, family, education, talent, and passion. Nature is aristocratic. The normal man is a fiction, al-

though certain generally valid laws do exist. Psychic life is a development that can easily be arrested on the lowest levels. It is as though every individual had a specific gravity, in accordance with which he either rises, or sinks down, to the level where he reaches his limit. His views and convictions will be determined accordingly. No wonder, then, that by far the greater number of marriages reach their upper psychological limit in fulfilment of the biological aim, without injury to spiritual or moral health. Relatively few people fall into deeper disharmony with themselves. Where there is a great deal of pressure from outside, the conflict is unable to develop much dramatic tension for sheer lack of energy. Psychological insecurity, however, increases in proportion to social security, unconsciously at first, causing neuroses, then consciously, bringing with it separations, discord, divorces, and other marital disorders. On still higher levels, new possibilities of psychological development are discerned, touching on the sphere of religion where critical judgment comes to a halt.

344   Progress may be permanently arrested on any of these levels, with complete unconsciousness of what might have followed at the next stage of development. As a rule graduation to the next stage is barred by violent prejudices and superstitious fears. This, however, serves a most useful purpose, since a man who is compelled by accident to live at a level too high for him becomes a fool and a menace.

345   Nature is not only aristocratic, she is also esoteric. Yet no man of understanding will thereby be induced to make a secret of what he knows, for he realizes only too well that the secret of psychic development can never be betrayed, simply because that development is a question of individual capacity.

BIBLIOGRAPHICAL NOTE
AND
INDEX

BIBLIOGRAPHICAL NOTE

In this volume, the footnote references to Professor Jung's publications cite the volumes of the *Collected Works* in which the writings appear. As, however, a considerable time will elapse before some of the volumes in question are published, additional references are given to extant versions to which the reader may refer. These alternate versions are listed below, in alphabetical order. The full contents of the *Collected Works* are announced at the end of the present volume.

"Archetypes of the Collective Unconscious," Vol. 9, part i.
  The Integration of the Personality, trans. by Stanley M. Dell (New York, 1939; London, 1940), pp. 52–95.

"The Association Method," Vol. 2, part ii.
  Trans. by A. A. Brill in *Collected Papers on Analytical Psychology* (2nd ed., London, 1917; New York, 1920), pp. 94–155.

"Mind and Earth," Vol. 10.
  Contributions to Analytical Psychology, trans. by H. G. and Cary F. Baynes (London and New York, 1928), pp. 99–140.

"Paracelsus as a Spiritual Phenomenon," Vol. 13.
  "Paracelsus als geistige Erscheinung," in *Paracelsica* (Zurich, 1942), pp. 43–176.

"Psychological Aspects of the Mother Archetype," Vol. 9, part i.
  "Die psychologischen Aspekte des Mutterarchetypus," *Eranos-Jahrbuch 1938* (Zurich, 1939), 403–43.

"The Psychology of the Child Archetype" and "The Psychological Aspects of the Kore," Vol. 9, part i.

> C. G. Jung and C. Kerényi, *Essays on a Science of Mythology,* trans. by R. F. C. Hull (Bollingen Series XXII, New York, 1949; entitled *Introduction to a Science of Mythology,* London, 1950), pp. 95–138, 215–45.

"On the Psychology and Pathology of So-called Occult Phenomena," Vol. 1.

> Trans. by M. D. Eder in *Collected Papers on Analytical Psychology* (2nd ed., London, 1917; New York, 1920), pp. 1–93.

"The Psychology of Dementia Praecox," Vol. 3.

> *The Psychology of Dementia Praecox,* trans. by A. A. Brill, Nervous and Mental Disease Monograph Series No. 3 (New York and Washington, 1936).

"A Review of the Complex Theory," Vol. 8.

> "Allgemeines zur Komplextheorie," in *Über psychische Energetik und das Wesen der Träume* (Zurich, 1948), pp. 119–44.

"Spirit and Life," Vol. 8.

> *Contributions to Analytical Psychology,* trans. by H. G. and Cary F. Baynes (London and New York, 1928), pp. 77–98.

Studies in Word Association, Vol. 2

> C. G. Jung and others, *Studies in Word Association,* trans. by M. D. Eder (London, 1918; New York, 1919), pp. 8–172, 206–65, 297–321, 354–406.

Symbols of Transformation, Vol. 5.

> *Symbole der Wandlung* (Zurich, 1952). This is a greatly revised version of *The Psychology of the Unconscious,* trans. by Beatrice Hinkle (New York, 1916; London, 1917).

INDEX

A

consciousness (*cont.*):

ated by psyche, 90; development of, 68, 75, 119, 190; — in child, 52; disintegration of, 153; an end-result, 52; extension of, 190; individual, basis of, 179; —, a superstructure on collective unconscious, 117; ineffectual compared to unconscious, 42; normal, 51; over-valuation of, 200; as self-cognition of universe, 90; sudden flashes of, 116; threshold of potential, 108; *see also* ego; unconscious

constipation, 73

constitution: inherited, 131; psychopathic, 141

contagion: by example, 150; unconscious, 150

"contained" and "container," 195*ff*

contemplation, 116

convention(s), 174*f*, 178; a collective necessity, 174; mechanism of, 179

convulsions, 73; *see also* epilepsy

creative work, and disease, 115

criminality, 43, 72; habitual, 70

Cromwell, Oliver, 83

cruelty, and sadism, 75

cryptomnesia, 110

culture: adult as upholder of, 58; aetiological c.-myth, 111; contemporary, 12*n*, 111, 177, 185, 197; = continuity, 144; c.-creating spirit, 85; creation of, 111, 114; cultural man, 86; meaning of, 85; teacher and, 58

curriculum, school, 144, 152

customs, observance of, cloak for a lie, 40

D

daemon, 141, 175; personal, of heroes, 175; private, 176; of Socrates, 176; voice of, 176; *see also* demons

danger, 61; snake symbol of, 125

daughter, 125; individuality of, 128

daydreaming, 105, 138

death, 9, 11, 15, 61; child's concept of, 9, 11; dreams of, 128; of mother, 11, 128

defectives, pathological, 172; *see also* imbeciles; mental defectives

degeneration, pathological, 151

deification of hero figures, 181

delusions, 145

dementia praecox: and analysis, 24; fear of father in, 26

demons, 116; *see also* daemon; devil

dependence, state of, 58

depression, 73

desert (dream-image), 118

development: collective, 174; embryonic, 53; neurotic, 95; spiritual, 194; —, resistance to, 159

devil, 180; concretism of the, 182; as objective psyche, 180; *see also* demons

diagnosis, 107, 132

dictatorship, 167, 168*n*

digestive disturbances, 73

disappointments, professional, 57

discontent, cultural, 111

disease(s): and creation, 115; as *entia*, 113

disintegration, 197, 200

displacement, 163

dissociation, 114, 196; tendency to, 194*f*

distortion, dream mechanism of, 163

divine, experience of the, 192

divorce, 123, 201

doctor: advice and reproof by, 96; desirable for analysis, 154; empirical and psychological outlook, 86; as father surrogate, 84*f*; and misunderstandings, 97; personality of, 140; *see also* analyst

doll(s), 23*f*; as grandmother, 27; children as, 127

double, psychic, 131; *see also* personality

inattentiveness, 138
incarnation, of ancestral spirit, 45
incest, 126; misleading use of term, 75; unconscious, 125; *see also* fantasies
incubation period, 110
indecision, neurotic, 76
independence of mind, importance of, 94
Indians, South American, 34
individual, 171; capacity, 201; embryonic development of, 53; a new experiment of life, 93; and species, 192; a unique combination of psychic elements, 93; *see also* child(ren)
individualism, 173, 175
individuality, 97; child as, 44; child's, and ancestors, 44; — not derived from parents' psyche, 44; of daughter, 128
individuation, 179
indolence, 105; *see also* laziness
ineducability, 151f
inertia, 105
infantilism, 158, 162; of adult, 168
inferiority: feeling of, 121f, in child, 130; moral, 130, 141
inflation, 142
inheritance, *see* heredity
initiation: ceremonies, 85, 159; into manhood, 160f; of treatment, 160
inner life: of child, 54; of neurotic, 183
inner voice, *see* voice
innocents, massacre of, 186
insanity, 97, 116, 149; moral, 70f
insecurity, 201
insight, flashes of, 45
inspirations, fantasies as, 105
instinct(s), 53, 158, 191f, 197; aesthetic, in animals, 83; balance of, 81; distinction between, 83; overvaluation of, 84; religious, 83; repressed/repression of, 15n, 105; restrictions on, 82; sexual, Freud and, 81

integration, inner, 197
intellect, 107, 177; and feeling-values, 100; precocious, 139
intelligence: suspicion of, 137; i. tests, 121, 129
intentions: good, 131; real, 101
interest(s): abnormal, 138; aesthetic, 105, 162; intellectual, 162; object of, 109; religious, 162
International Congress of Education, 49n, 63, 149
interpretation, 15n; Freudian, 3, 105; sexual, 106; *see also* dream-interpretation
introversion, 13&n, 16
inversion, 163
irrational values, 40
Italy, 20, 167
ivory figure, Japanese, 160, 161

J

Jacobi, Jolande, 113n
Janet, Pierre, 66, 68
jealousy, 121
Jesus, 180, 181; in Protestantism, 181; Temptation of, 180, 184; vocation of, 180
Jews: and circumcision, 161; and Messiah, 180
Jordan, Pascual, 89n
Josephus, Flavius, 155
judgments, individual, 151
Jung, Carl Gustav: school reminiscence, 136
CASES IN SUMMARY *(in order of presentation, numbered for reference):*
[1] Anna, aged 3, subject of "Psychic Conflicts in a Child." — 9–35
[2] Girl, aged 15, who harboured an unconscious fantasy of mother's death. — 11
[3] Boy, who dreamed the erotic and religious problems of father (ref.). — 53

T

V

vacuum, psychic, 101
values: collective, and individual uniqueness, 150; irrational, of child, 40; moral, 40; spiritual, 40
verbal facility, 139
virgin (dream-image), 118
virtue, rooted in vice, 106
vision(s): fantasies as, 105; madman's, 116; of nun, 72; symbolism of, 106; *see also* dream(s); fantasy(-ies)
vocation, 175*ff*; and collective necessities, 176; feeling of, 176; as psychic necessity, 178; sacrifice of self to, 180; and voice of inner man, 176
voice: of God, 116; inner, 176*ff*; —, and ego, 185; —, and evil, 184*f*; —, and Lucifer, 185; —, and neurosis, 183; tone of, 14
volcanoes, 17, 18, 20

W

Wagner, Richard, 115
walking, uncoordinated, 121
wars, as psychic epidemics, 177*f*; *see also* World War, first
wedding ring, *see* ring
well (dream-image), 156*f*

whole man, 107, 143
wholeness, 170*f*, 174, 179, 183; individual and group, 176
Wickes, Frances G., 39*ff*, 121
will: acrobatics of, 174; division of, 194; a phenomenon, 91; and psychic contents, 91; will to power, mother's, 126*f*
wings (dream-image), 61
wish(es), 182; egoistic, 23
wish-fulfilment, 20, 163; dream as, 100*f*, 103, 128*n*, *see also* dream(s)
witch, 55; witchcraft, 116
Wolff, Toni, 90*n*
woman: elderly (dream-figure), 160*f*; eternal image of, 198; masculine, 127; as mother, 192; woman-hater, 77
womb: of Church, 158; return to, 192
wood, fantasy of planing, 29
World War, first, 95
writing, 129, 132
Wundt, Wilhelm, 51
Wylie, Elinor, 199*n*
Wyss, Walter H. von, 83*n*

Y

young people, and marriage motives, 190; *see also* adolescence

The Collected Works of C. G. Jung

THE COLLECTED WORKS OF
C. G. JUNG

THE PUBLICATION of the first complete collected edition, in English, of the works of C. G. Jung has been undertaken by Routledge and Kegan Paul, Ltd., in England and by the Bollingen Foundation, Inc., through Pantheon Books, Inc., in the United States. The edition contains revised versions of works previously published, such as *The Psychology of the Unconscious*, now entitled *Symbols of Transformation;* works originally written in English, such as *Psychology and Religion;* works not previously translated, such as the *Mysterium Coniunctionis;* and, in general, new translations of the major body of Professor Jung's writings. The author has supervised the textual revision, which in some cases is extensive. Sir Herbert Read, Dr. Michael Fordham, and Dr. Gerhard Adler compose the Editorial Committee; the translator is R. F. C. Hull.

Every volume of the Collected Works contains material that either has not previously been published in English or is being newly published in revised form. In addition to the *Mysterium Coniunctionis,* the following volumes will in large part be new to English readers: *Psychiatric Studies; Archetypes and the Collective Unconscious; Alchemical Studies; The Spirit in Man, Art, and Literature;* and *The Practice of Psychotherapy.*

The volumes are not necessarily being published in consecutive order, but, generally speaking, new works of which translations are lacking are being given precedence. The price of the volumes varies according to size; they are sold separately, and may also be ordered as a set. In the following pages the volumes of the Collected Works are listed together with their contents, as now arranged. Each volume will also contain an index and, in most cases, a bibliography; the final volume will contain a complete bibliography of Professor Jung's writings and a general index of the entire edition. Subsequent works of the author's will be added in due course.

1. PSYCHIATRIC STUDIES
On the Psychology and Pathology of So-Called Occult Phenomena: A Psychiatric Study
A Case of Hysterical Stupor in a Prisoner Awaiting Trial
On Manic Alteration
On Simulated Insanity
A Medical Opinion on a Case of Simulated Insanity
On Hysterical Parapraxes in Reading
Cryptomnesia
A Third and Conclusive Opinion on Two Contradictory Psychiatric Diagnoses
On the Psychological Determination of Facts

2. EXPERIMENTAL RESEARCHES (BOUND IN TWO PARTS)
PART I
STUDIES IN WORD ASSOCIATION
The Association of Normal Subjects (by Jung and Riklin)
Experimental Observations on Memory
On the Determination of Facts by Psychological Means
Analysis of the Associations of an Epileptic
PART II
STUDIES IN WORD ASSOCIATION (*continued*)
The Association Method
Reaction-Time in Association Experiments
On Disturbances in Reproduction in Association Experiments
The Significance of Association Experiments for Psychopathology
Psychoanalysis and Association Experiments
Association, Dream, and Hysterical Symptoms
PSYCHOPHYSICAL RESEARCHES
On Psychophysical Relations of the Association Experiment
Psychophysical Investigations with the Galvanometer and Pneumograph in Normal and Insane Individuals (by Peterson and Jung)

(*continued*)

* A revision of *The Psychology of the Unconscious.*

* Published 1953.

                                            (continued)

* Published 1953.

Sigmund Freud: A Cultural Phenomenon
Sigmund Freud: An Obituary
Richard Wilhelm: An Obituary
Psychology and Literature
On the Relation of Analytical Psychology to the Poetic Art
Picasso
"Ulysses"

16. THE PRACTICE OF PSYCHOTHERAPY *
ESSAYS ON THE PSYCHOLOGY OF THE
TRANSFERENCE AND OTHER SUBJECTS
    GENERAL PROBLEMS OF PSYCHOTHERAPY
Principles of Practical Psychotherapy
What Is Psychotherapy?
Some Aspects of Modern Psychotherapy
Aims of Modern Psychotherapy
Problems of Modern Psychotherapy
Psychotherapy and a Philosophy of Life
Medicine and Psychotherapy
Psychotherapy Today
Fundamental Questions of Psychotherapy
    SPECIFIC PROBLEMS OF PSYCHOTHERAPY
The Therapeutic Value of Abreaction
The Practical Use of Dream Analysis
Psychology of the Transference

17. THE DEVELOPMENT OF PERSONALITY *
Psychic Conflicts in a Child
Introduction to Wickes's "Analyse der Kinderseele"
Child Development and Education
Analytical Psychology and Education: Three Lectures
The Gifted Child
The Significance of the Unconscious in Individual Education
The Development of Personality
Marriage as a Psychological Relationship

FINAL VOLUME: MISCELLANEOUS WORKS,
BIBLIOGRAPHY, AND GENERAL INDEX
        REVIEWS, SHORT ARTICLES, ETC., OF THE PSYCHOANALYTICAL
            PERIOD
        LATER INTRODUCTIONS, ETC.
        BIBLIOGRAPHY OF C. G. JUNG'S WRITINGS
        GENERAL INDEX OF THE COLLECTED WORKS
* Published 1954.